UNDERSTANDING
LOUISE ERDRICH

UNDERSTANDING CONTEMPORARY AMERICAN LITERATURE

Matthew J. Bruccoli, Founding Editor

Linda Wagner-Martin, Series Editor

Volumes on

Edward Albee | Sherman Alexie | Nelson Algren | Paul Auster
Nicholson Baker | John Barth | Donald Barthelme | The Beats
Thomas Berger | The Black Mountain Poets | Robert Bly | T. C. Boyle
Truman Capote | Raymond Carver | Michael Chabon | Fred Chappell
Chicano Literature | Contemporary American Drama
Contemporary American Horror Fiction
Contemporary American Literary Theory
Contemporary American Science Fiction, 1926–1970
Contemporary American Science Fiction, 1970–2000
Contemporary Chicana Literature | Pat Conroy | Robert Coover | Don DeLillo
Philip K. Dick | James Dickey | E. L. Doctorow | Rita Dove | Dave Eggers
Louise Erdrich | John Gardner | George Garrett | Tim Gautreaux | John Hawkes
Joseph Heller | Lillian Hellman | Beth Henley | James Leo Herlihy | David Henry Hwang
John Irving | Randall Jarrell | Gish Jen | Charles Johnson | Diane Johnson
Adrienne Kennedy | William Kennedy | Jack Kerouac | Jamaica Kincaid
Etheridge Knight | Tony Kushner | Ursula K. Le Guin | Jonathan Lethem
Denise Levertov | Bernard Malamud | David Mamet | Bobbie Ann Mason
Colum McCann | Cormac McCarthy | Jill McCorkle | Carson McCullers
W. S. Merwin | Arthur Miller | Stephen Millhauser | Lorrie Moore
Toni Morrison's Fiction | Vladimir Nabokov | Gloria Naylor | Joyce Carol Oates
Tim O'Brien | Flannery O'Connor | Cynthia Ozick | Suzan-Lori Parks | Walker Percy
Katherine Anne Porter | Richard Powers | Reynolds Price | Annie Proulx
Thomas Pynchon | Theodore Roethke | Philip Roth | Richard Russo | May Sarton
Hubert Selby, Jr. | Mary Lee Settle | Sam Shepard | Neil Simon
Isaac Bashevis Singer | Jane Smiley | Gary Snyder | William Stafford
Robert Stone | Anne Tyler | Gerald Vizenor | Kurt Vonnegut
David Foster Wallace | Robert Penn Warren | James Welch | Eudora Welty
Edmund White | Colson Whitehead | Tennessee Williams
August Wilson | Charles Wright

UNDERSTANDING LOUISE ERDRICH

Seema Kurup

The University of South Carolina Press

Published by the University of South Carolina Press
Columbia, South Carolina 29208

www.sc.edu/uscpress

Manufactured in the United States of America

25 24 23 22 21 20 19 18 17 16
10 9 8 7 6 5 4 3 2 1

Library of Congress Cataloging-in-Publication Data
can be found at http://catalog.loc.gov/.

ISBN 978-1-61117-623-0 (cloth)
ISBN 978-1-61117-624-7 (ebook)

This book was printed on recycled paper with
30 percent postconsumer waste content.

This book is dedicated, as is all my life's good works,
to my beloved parents, Dr. Siva Prasad Kurup and Usha Kurup,
to whom I owe everything and without whom I am nothing.

CONTENTS

SERIES EDITOR'S PREFACE

The Understanding Contemporary American Literature series was founded by the estimable Matthew J. Bruccoli (1931–2008), who envisioned these volumes as guides or companions for students as well as good nonacademic readers, a legacy that will continue as new volumes are developed to fill in gaps among the nearly one hundred series volumes published to date and to embrace a host of new writers only now making their marks on our literature.

As Professor Bruccoli explained in his preface to the volumes he edited, because much influential contemporary literature makes special demands, "the word understanding in the titles was chosen deliberately. Many willing readers lack an adequate understanding of how contemporary literature works; that is, of what the author is attempting to express and the means by which it is conveyed." Aimed at fostering this understanding of good literature and good writers, the criticism and analysis in the series provide instruction in how to read certain contemporary writers—explicating their material, language, structures, themes, and perspectives– and facilitate a more profitable experience of the works under discussion.

In the twenty-first century Professor Bruccoli's prescience gives us an avenue to publish expert critiques of significant contemporary American writing. The series continues to map the literary landscape and to provide both instruction and enjoyment. Future volumes will seek to introduce new voices alongside canonized favorites, to chronicle the changing literature of our times, and to remain, as Professor Bruccoli conceived, contemporary in the best sense of the word.

Linda Wagner-Martin, Series Editor

ACKNOWLEDGMENTS

I owe my undying gratitude to my dearest family for their unwavering love and edifying encouragement: my late paternal grandparents, Vasudevan and Subhadra Kurup; my maternal grandparents, Ramachandran and the late Lakshmi Vellodi; my aunts, Dr. Shanta Kurup and Suvarna Nair; my Nair cousins, nephews, and nieces; my uncle and aunt Dilip and Amritha Vellodi; and my Vellodi cousins. Special loving thanks to my beloved Kurt Neumann and to my dear friends Chris Padgett, Catherine Restovich and Patti Ferguson for their unwavering love and bolstering daily support. Thanks to my sweet Baron, for keeping my feet warm under the kitchen table as I pounded away on my computer instead of walking him.

Sincere thanks also goes to Prof. Wayne Kvam for introducing me to Louise Erdrich's work and giving me the priceless gift of self-confidence and to the faculty and administration at William Rainey Harper College for awarding me a sabbatical to finish my project. Thanks also to the University of South Carolina Press staff and editors, and special thanks to Jim Denton and series editor Prof. Linda Wagner-Martin for their patience, support, and the opportunity to share my understanding of Erdrich's work.

Gitchi-Migwetch goes to Louise Erdrich for her words—every single one. Thank God, Gizhe Manidoo, for everything.

CHAPTER 1

Understanding Louise Erdrich

Karen Louise Erdrich was born in Little Falls, Minnesota, on June 7, 1954, to Rita Joanne Gourneau, enrolled member of the Turtle Mountain Band of Ojibwe, and Ralph Louis Erdrich, the son of German immigrants. Both of her parents were teachers at a school run by the Bureau of Indian Affairs (BIA) in Wahpeton, North Dakota, where Erdrich, the eldest of their seven children, was raised.[1] Wahpeton sits in the Red River Valley along the North Dakota–Minnesota border, and fictionalized versions of the town provide the setting of many of Erdrich's novels, revealing the profound impact this midwestern landscape had on her. Growing up, she was also exposed to and immersed in both sides of her rich cultural heritage—Ojibwe and Euro-American. As a child she found herself enchanted with the mysticism and mystery of the Old Testament: "I was at the age of magical thinking and believed sticks could change to serpents, a voice might speak from a burning bush, angels wrestled with people. After I went to school and started catechism I realized religion was about rules. I remember staring at a neighbor's bridal-wreath bush. It bloomed every year but was voiceless. No angels, no parting of the Red River. It all seemed so dull once I realized that nothing spectacular was going to happen."[2] Other than her Old Testament fascination, Erdrich's early reading habits involved simply raiding the stacks of the local library "indiscriminately" for writers such as Leon Uris, James Michener, Ayn Rand, Herman Wouk, and James Welch, though she preferred John Tanner's *The Falcon,* William Shakespeare's plays, "the *Dune* trilogy, Isaac Asimov and *The Prophet*."[3] Erdrich came from a family of storytellers, so she lived a richly imaginative early life. One of her greatest early literary influences was her father, Ralph Erdrich. Erdrich explains, "My father is a terrific storyteller and made his relatives and the characters in the towns where he grew up almost mythic."[4] In addition to being an engaging storyteller who would often break into spontaneous poetic recitations of Henry Wadsworth Longfellow or Robert Frost, he encouraged Erdrich to pursue her own creative star. To give the budding young writer even greater incentive, he would pay his daughter a nickel for each piece of creative writing she composed.[5]

Erdrich also received the creative benefit of hearing family stories from both sides of her ancestry. The history of her paternal grandparents, Ludwig Friedrich Erdrich and Mary Kroll, a German immigrant butcher and his wife, ultimately inspired such novels as *The Beet Queen* (1986) and *The Master Butchers Singing Club* (2003) and "The Butcher's Wife" poems in her early poetry collections. Though Erdrich's German background is the focus of these important works, her authentic voice seems to come forth more naturally from her Ojibwe roots. Arguably her maternal grandparents, Patrice and Mary Gourneau, were a more significant influence on her literary work, which has as its primary focus the Ojibwe part of her heritage. Though raised Catholic, Erdrich was exposed to a great deal of Ojibwe culture: she heard traditional stories, participated in cultural ceremonies, and learned tribal history. Pat Gourneau was a prominent tribal elder and political activist for tribal rights. In describing the position of Gourneau in the family, Erdrich explained, "He's kind of a legend in our family. He is funny, he's charming, he's interesting. He, for many years, was a very strong figure in my life. I guess I idolized him. A very intelligent man."[6] Gourneau was not only a beloved grandfather but also an undeniable force in the community. He served as the tribal chairman for the Ojibwe tribe on the Turtle Mountain reservation in North Dakota during the 1950s, when the U.S. government devised a solution called "termination" as a remedy to the "Indian problem."[7] Termination was designed to undo the relationship between the federal government and Native Americans, so individual tribes would be forced to dissolve and join mainstream American society. The policy would have transferred communal tribal land held by the reservation into privately owned parcels for sale—in essence taking away the Ojibwe's most prized possession. Erdrich explained the motivation behind her grandfather's tireless fight against this policy: "He recognized that this would be the end of the Turtle Mountain Chippewa as a people."[8] After Gourneau testified before Congress to ensure his reservation would be exempt, the tribe avoided a frenzied sell-off, which preserved the reservation and saved the tribe from possible extinction. Gourneau's efforts impressed upon Erdrich the critical relationship between Ojibwe survival and the land. Keenly aware of her grandfather's legacy growing up, she committed herself to telling the story of the Ojibwe people, since remembering through storytelling is a traditional and time-honored form of preserving Ojibwe heritage. Recognizing Erdrich's compassion and respect for the Ojibwe and the sacred view of the land embraced by her Anishinaabe ancestors is essential to understanding her body of work.

Erdrich's educational background includes a bachelor of arts in 1976 from Dartmouth College, where she was part of the first class of women to gain admission to the college. Far from her hometown of Wahpeton and attending an Ivy League school, with all of the attendant cultural and social norms of New England, Erdrich faced an authentic culture shock and intense adjustment period. She admits her success was due to the kindness of instructors, advisers, and the community of Native American scholars at Dartmouth, who took under their collective wing the "wide-eyed, chainsmoking, wild-haired, disorganized, red-booted young woman from North Dakota, and managed, with their love and examples, to bring me through."[9] Among those generous individuals was Michael Dorris, chairman of the newly established Native American Studies program and an instructor in the department. Erdrich extolls Dorris's contribution to the program and to those Native American scholars, like herself, who joined the nascent program: "He gave himself utterly to the task, and used his tough humor, tenacity, and courage to make sure the program and the department would be of ongoing integrity. So it continues. Without him, there would be no voices to collect."[10] Dorris eventually became Erdrich's husband, and together they created one of the most celebrated literary partnerships of the late twentieth century.

The Dartmouth years, then, significantly altered the course of Erdrich's life and career, but not only because of Dorris. Dartmouth's Native American Studies program offered a young Erdrich the opportunity to explore, cultivate, and refine her Ojibwe voice. Along with the other students in the program, Erdrich developed a "reliance on community and an appreciation of the blessings of connection."[11] Decidedly these two themes, community and connection, are central to Erdrich's literary work—the communities of the fictional Argus, Hoopdance, and Little No Horse figure in almost all of her novels, and connections of kinship and genealogical ties abound in her stories. Though Dartmouth's Native American students were of different tribal backgrounds, both mixed-blood and full-blood, there was a common need shared among them in terms of identity: "the need to integrate, a need to make sense of a world that does not include them, a need to return to places deeply longed for and understood."[12] The creation of a cultural identity, the struggles of tribal members and their communities to belong in the world at large, and the overwhelming pull of place, of home, take up much of the striving and conflict in Erdrich's work. Her time at Dartmouth precipitated an enriching and liberating seismic shift in her world that would irrevocably affect her art and her life.

After graduating from Dartmouth, Erdrich remained in New England for a time before returning to North Dakota. Eventually the call to pursue her creative writing talents led her back east to graduate studies at Johns Hopkins University, where she had the opportunity to study under various literary luminaries, including John Barth, Edmund White, Richard Howard, and C. Michael Curtis.[13] Upon receiving her master of fine arts degree in 1979, Erdrich ultimately returned to Dartmouth as a writer-in-residence, where her professional relationship with Dorris, who had remained in contact with her, evolved into a romantic one; they married in 1981. Erdrich settled in New Hampshire with Dorris and his three adopted children, Reynold Abel, Jeffrey Sava, and Madeline, whom Dorris had previously adopted while single. During the course of their nearly seventeen-year marriage, Erdrich gave birth to three daughters, Persia, Pallas, and Aza, all while embarking in earnest on a literary career. Dorris, a writer himself, published a number of works, including *A Yellow Raft in Blue Water* (1987), and received the 1989 National Book Critics Circle Award for his critically acclaimed memoir, *The Broken Cord: A Family's Ongoing Struggle with Fetal Alcohol Syndrome,* which includes a foreword by Erdrich. The book describes the condition known as fetal alcohol syndrome, which afflicted their adopted son Reynold, who died after being struck by a car in a hit-and-run accident.

Erdrich and Dorris's literary partnership became the subject of public admiration and fascination. They collaborated on a number of early stories and books; throughout their relationship Dorris supported Erdrich professionally as a trusted adviser, literary agent, editor, tireless promoter, and sounding board. On his suggestion a reluctant Erdrich entered the short story "The World's Greatest Fisherman" in the competition for the Nelson Algren Literary Award, which she won. The story became the first chapter of the novel *Love Medicine* (1984), winner of the National Book Critics Circle Award for fiction. Her poetry was gaining critical attention at this time, as well, with the publication of *Jacklight* (1984) and *Baptism of Desire* (1989), parts of which appear with newer poems in *Original Fire: New and Selected Poems* (2003). Though some of Erdrich's early works, parts of *Love Medicine* (1984) and the coauthored *The Crown of Columbus* (1991) and *Route 2* (1991), were written in collaboration with Dorris, there is some confusion about which other of her novels were the product of shared creative effort. The task to parse who authored what portions of the early novels, including *The Beet Queen* (1986), a finalist for the National Book Critics Circle Award, *Tracks* (1988), and *The Bingo Palace* (1994), would be impossible. Indeed early interviews with Erdrich failed to clarify the extent and depth of their joint efforts: "In the course of it [the writing of a novel], we'll continuously plot and continuously talk about who the characters are, what they eat, what clothes they wear, what their favorite colors are and what's going to happen to them. In that way, I think it's a true kind of collaboration: we both really influence the course of the book. You can't look back and say which one made it go this way or that way, because you can't remember."[14] Of course, at that time Erdrich was a woman who loved her husband and the father of her children, admired him as a gifted educator, depended on him as her literary agent and first reader, and shared her writing with him as a trusted editor and adviser. Dorris was present at most of those early interviews, which number more than one hundred, and the pressure on Erdrich to maintain the impression that she and Dorris were engaged in a wholly collaborative literary partnership must have been compelling for a number of professional and personal reasons.

In the intervening years, particularly since Dorris's death, Erdrich has opened up about the collaboration in more candid terms. For those curious in learning more about the extent and the nature of their creative partnership, she has set the record straight: "I would have loved for Michael to have had his own life as a writer and not covet my life as a writer. But he couldn't help himself. So in agreeing to write *The Crown of Columbus* I really made a deal, at least in my thoughts, that if we wrote this one book together, then we could openly work separately—as we always did in truth, of course."[15] The early novels were published under Erdrich's name alone, officially crediting her as the sole author. There is no question that Erdrich valued Dorris as a keen and intuitive editor of her works, but the notion that her novels should actually be considered collaborations should be called into question, particularly as evidenced by her ongoing list of publications since 1997. In a 2012 interview promoting *The Round House,* Terry Tazioli asked Erdrich how different it was to write on her own compared to writing collaboratively with Dorris, and Erdrich gave a straightforward answer: "It's not any different. I wrote it all. . . . So, collaborating wasn't like . . . he would write a page and I would write a page. It was more that I had someone who gave me very, very wonderful editorial advice."[16] The Erdrich-Dorris literary partnership effectively came to an end in 1996 when the couple separated. Dorris committed suicide in 1997. The loss of Dorris left Erdrich a single mother and the focus of unwanted attention and speculation on the part of the literary community about her personal affairs.

During this difficult period in her life, Erdrich continued publishing novels regularly: *Tales of Burning Love* was published earlier in the same year as Dorris's death, followed by *The Antelope Wife* (1998). Erdrich continued her creative output with *The Last Report on the Miracles at Little No Horse* (2001), a finalist for the National Book Award; *The Master Butchers Singing Club* (2003); *Four Souls* (2004); and *The Painted Drum* (2005). After a brief hiatus,

Erdrich followed this stream of novels with another prolific period, publishing some of her most critically acclaimed novels—*The Plague of Doves* (2008), a finalist for the Pulitzer Prize; *Shadow Tag* (2009); and *The Round House* (2012), winner of the National Book Award—as well as *The Red Convertible: Collected and New Stories* (2009). In addition to her adult fiction and poetry, Erdrich has written an award-winning series of children's books that includes *The Birchbark House* (1999), *The Game of Silence* (2005), *The Porcupine Year* (2008), and *Chickadee* (2012). She has also written nonfiction, including a memoir of motherhood, *The Blue Jay's Dance* (1995), and *Books and Islands in Ojibwe Country* (2003), a memoir of her travels through Ojibwe country and a catalog of various cultural aspects of Ojibwe life.

Erdrich lives in Minneapolis, Minnesota, where she owns an independent bookstore, Birchbark Books, which specializes in Native American literature and Ojibwe-language publications. The bookstore proudly displays a handmade canoe hanging from the ceiling and an authentic confessional salvaged from an old church, in a nod to her Catholic heritage and perhaps a smirk from her Ojibwe self. In her continuing commitment to preserve Ojibwe language and culture, Erdrich established the Birchbark House Fund to support indigenous language revitalization and, with her sisters, formed the Wiigwaas Press to publish material in Ojibwe and bilingual Ojibwe/English. Paralleling her growing list of publications, Erdrich's family has expanded as well. She had a fourth daughter, Nenaa'ikiizhikok, in 2000, who is featured in *Books and Islands in Ojibwe Country,* and married a local businessman from Minneapolis, Dan Emmel, in 2008. Erdrich remains engaged with Ojibwe life and community: she continues her studies in the language, runs regular writing workshops with her sister Heid Erdrich, also a creative writer, and travels regularly to Ojibwe retreats and sacred places. During her acceptance speech at the 2013 North Dakota Theodore Roosevelt Rough Riders Awards ceremony, an honor bestowed to exceptional North Dakotans, Erdrich remembered her Ojibwe ancestors: "I want in this context to thank the old people who really sacrificed to keep alive Anishinaabe culture, ways, and language."[17] Clearly evidenced in her thanks to those Ojibwe who have gone before is Erdrich's unwavering commitment to preserve the fruits of their sacrifice.

Understanding the Literature of Louise Erdrich

Louise Erdrich has created a literature of place in her novels, short fiction, children's literature, poetry, and nonfiction. To put her work in a larger cultural context, Erdrich's is a literature of the land, of home, where identity is clearly constructed out of the climate, the seasons, the natural world, and Ojibwe tribal culture and tradition. Native American identity had to be radically renegotiated in this space when European traders and settlers, the *chimookomanag*, arrived in the New World.[18] A colonial identity had to be constructed because of this cataclysmic encroachment. And unlike the postcolonial circumstances of the populations of the Far East, the Indian subcontinent, Africa, the West Indies, and other historically colonized nations, the occupation for Native Americans has never ended. To be sure, the trappings of colonial rule remain in many of those countries, but the daily reminders of occupation—the vestiges of the loss of land and the fight for sovereignty—cannot be ignored by a Native American living in the United States. Shifting population boundaries, once limitless, foreclosed traditional Native American identity and greatly compromised the freedoms and liberties of the indigenous populations with the occupation of European colonists and, ultimately, American settlers. During this transitional time, there was great upheaval, as disease, famine, Christianity, and eventually the U.S. government and land allotment acts overwhelmed the Native American community. Erdrich's work reflects this shift in Ojibwe identity and history. The loss of land and culture devastated many in the Ojibwe community. Government allotments, land deeds, illegal taxes, and boarding schools became the new conditions of the land rather than tribal law, kinship, and community. In fact the bureaucratic U.S. government system, with its papers and documents, replaced the traditional tribal way of transacting and negotiating, which was through sacred verbal promises, the sincere exchange of gifts and goods, oral tradition, and storytelling.

Historically the plight of Native Americans has been largely ignored in mainstream American history and literature. The prevailing images of Native Americans have been limited to depictions of "cowboys and Indians," whoops and war paint, the noble savage, and the 1970s "Keep America Beautiful" public service announcement, with a tear rolling down the face of an actor impersonating a Native American. In the popular imagination, Native American history is obscured with scenes of the first Thanksgiving or neat little teepees peppering a vast and arid landscape. For Erdrich writing against these absurd and belittling stereotypes is a formidable task. Alternately there is no all-encompassing Native American identity; the term is a tidy and easily managed category by which vastly different groups of indigenous people, with distinct languages, beliefs, and traditions, have been grouped. Instead there is a Cherokee or Sioux or Ojibwe identity and attendant literature, and within those larger designations exist distinctive clans, communities, families, and individuals. The problem ethnic writers continually face, and one Erdrich has had to contend with, is the pressure to provide a general and accurate representation of "their people" for popular consumption by the dominant culture. Identity is a fluid construction, not a fixed material reality. The facile picture of the noble savage or the victimized primitive has served for centuries as the all-encompassing symbol of the Native American.[19] This two-dimensional depiction aims to give non–Native Americans a definitive understanding of tribal and reservation life. It is a ridiculous assumption that one or two stock characters—who generally speak broken English, if they speak at all, and never seem to feel the normal human range of emotions, such as joy, love, nostalgia, loneliness, rage, and pain—could ever offer a rich enough vision of this complex and diverse people and their culture. Erdrich questions the idealized version of Native Americans that is perpetuated by the commonly romanticized and, in fact, unrealistic portrait of unique tribal peoples. She regularly subverts the dominant culture's desire to find the grand, totalizing narrative of Native American identity by offering competing small narratives in most all of her work to date; this move is a signature of her distinctive narrative style.

Narrative Style

Erdrich's work is peopled with various storytellers and their stories—deeply felt, personal accounts of events, people, and places in a central geographical community in Ojibwe country. Obviously this feature of Erdrich's writing is not exceptional—a narrative generally tells a story with an implied or explicit narrator. What makes her writing unique is the presence of multiple narrators, with their often competing narratives, occurring within the space of a single text. More problematic for Erdrich's first-time readers is reconciling the assortment of stories, which are regularly at odds with one another or focused on a singular, subjective aspect of the plot. Consequently an ordered sense of plot is often elusive in Erdrich's work, hard to pin down and rein in. For unaccustomed, beginning, or casual readers, her narrative style can be challenging and engaging or even confusing and frustrating. Indeed some early critics of Erdrich's novels dismissed her style as intentionally confounding, privileging an academic and experimental style rather than a substantive, politically engaged, and meaningful one.

The most infamous of these critiques is Leslie Marmon Silko's review of *The Beet Queen* titled "Here's an Odd Artifact for the Fairy Tale Shelf." Silko, the Laguna-Pueblo author of the critically acclaimed *Ceremony* (1977) and a central figure in the renaissance of Native American literature in the 1970s and '80s, leveled the claim of insensitive, ivory-tower disengagement against Erdrich: "[her] prose is an outgrowth of academic, post-modern, so called experimental influences. The idea is to 'set language free,' to allow words to interact like magical chemicals in a word sorcerer's pristine laboratory, where a word and its possible relationship with other words may be seen 'as they really are, in and of themselves,' without the tiresome interference of any historical, political or cultural connections the words may have had in the past."[20] Silko's tirade continues, but the focus shifts from an attack on Erdrich's novel to a general screed against postmodern writing and its ineffectiveness in conveying political messages or acting as an appropriate vehicle by which issues of identity politics can be expressed: "Self-referential writing has an ethereal clarity and shimmering beauty because no history or politics intrudes to muddy the well of pure necessity contained within language itself. Post-modern, self-referential writing reflects the isolation and alienation of the individual who shares nothing in common with other human beings but language and its hygienic grammatical mechanisms. Self-referential writing is light years away from shared or communal experience that underlies oral narrative and modern fiction."[21] Silko misreads postmodern strategies as antithetical to identity politics, declaring categorically that they are inappropriate for an ethnic writer to adopt and adapt. She fails to acknowledge postmodern fiction's inherent questioning of power relations, idealized versions of history, and the objectivity of totalizing narratives; postmodern fictional strategies provide the disenfranchised writer a space to renegotiate, recast, and interrogate subjugating narratives of the past. An interesting aside, and a glaring irony, is that Silko's own novel *Ceremony* appears, in abridged form, in the Norton anthology *Postmodern American Fiction* (1997) while none of Erdrich's works is included.

In their collection of interviews with Erdrich and Dorris, Allan and Nancy Feyl Chavkin ask Erdrich what might account for Silko's extreme response; Erdrich at first playfully responds, "Drugs." She goes on, though, to speculate that Silko misunderstood that the German part of her ancestry was the intended focus of *The Beet Queen:* "Honestly, here's what I think happened. Leslie Silko didn't read the book carefully. It happens. I've done it myself. She thought the main characters were Chippewa when they were actually depression-era Poles and Germans. It is no wonder she wrote a diatribe. They must have seemed shockingly assimilated."[22] Although it is unlikely that Silko mistook the European immigrant characters for Native Americans, Erdrich graciously dispelled any notions of a brewing feud between the two authors by dismissing the review as a misunderstanding. Susan Pérez Castillo argues that "it is possible that some of her [Silko's] differences with Erdrich arise from misunderstandings related to a limited concept of ethnicity, and an essentialist, logocentric view of referentiality" rather than an intentional meanness or petty jealousy.[23] Silko and Erdrich simply have profoundly different perspectives on the nature of representation and how it operates in Native American literature.

Writers must deal from time to time with public criticism, of course, and Erdrich's reviewers have sometimes, though not often, been lukewarm in their reception of this or that work. To date, however, Silko's review remains the most scathing review of Erdrich's career, though it does open up the discussion of artistic choice (form) and its relation to ideological matters (content). Another takeaway of value in the review is an opportunity to explore the question of Erdrich's political engagement. Her writing is politically charged; moreover through her distinctive narrative style, particularly the use of multiple narrators, she reflects the history and politics of the Ojibwe arguably more effectively than she could writing in the tradition of Western realism. Only through an exploration and interrogation of the many fictions of the Ojibwe can Erdrich begin to deconstruct the received grand narrative of Native American identity and reconstruct a fair, authentic representation of the Ojibwe. And through this reconstruction Erdrich arrives at a world that comprises a myriad of individual subjectivities that do not claim to know the whole truth but regional, local, and personal truths, which are equally valuable and viable in constructing a portrait of her Ojibwe community and their history. Any claim to grand narratives is fueled by ideology, hubris, and delusion rather than lived reality. Erdrich steers clear of any such notion that her fiction and poetry can speak for the whole of the Ojibwe people or the greater Native American community. It is only those who wish to pigeonhole that would lay claim to a static and fully reliable representation of a people. The constructions of ethnicity, cultural identity, and history are largely determined by the dominant culture and by those in power. Often cultural tags, such as "Native American," "woman," and "black," are meant only to oppress and subjugate rather than disclose a fluidity and fullness of being. Nancy J. Peterson observes that "for writers such as Erdrich . . . the history of America has often been exclusionary—a monologic narrative of male Anglo-American progress that constructs others as people without history." In light of this, Peterson concludes that "writing history . . . has become one way for marginalized peoples to counter their invisibility."[24] The historical record is said to be written by the "winners," so Erdrich offers an alternate, revisionist history that questions and critiques the historical representations of her people. In the popular imagination, Native Americans, living cloistered lives on their reservations, merely add to the biological landscape like the wildlife, which suggests an absence rather than a presence on the scale of intellectual, artistic, or emotional pursuits. Mainstream America must imagine that since colonization the various indigenous tribes comprise cheerful denizens of isolated Native American communities, simpleminded and lacking in sophistication, blissfully and ignorantly living out their days.

Where the Ojibwe were absent in the official story of history, Erdrich casts the tribe as a presence rather than an absence in the history of the United States and in contemporary life. In what Gerald Vizenor calls the literature of survivance, an effort to portray perseverance and survival, Native American authors practice a form of resistance through storytelling, which depicts Native American characters as engaged participants in the history and culture of North America; they continue to survive colonialism and are not simply tragic victims or ignorant savages.[25] Native American history, as well as identity, is perpetuated through its discourse, its stories; it is a communal narrative of events that serves to protect and preserve the culture and tradition. Pérez Castillo describes Erdrich's Ojibwe "not as Noble Savage victims or as dying representatives of a lost authenticity, but as tough, compassionate people who use the vital capacity of discourse to shape—and not merely reflect—reality."[26] The stories her characters share, in the form of oral histories, local myths, and family fictions, often create a contestable version of events. In order to offer a "realistic" version of Ojibwe existence, Erdrich effectively uses multiple narrators that act as buffers for one another. By not privileging one narrative over any other—no narrator/speaker can claim absolute authenticity or authority—Erdrich creates texts that reflect the diversity and often diametrically opposed realities of Ojibwe life. By using distinct, at times conflicting, narratives within a single text, Erdrich creates a tension similar to that surrounding the crisis of history and identity, a true struggle for survival that the Ojibwe experienced particularly in the late nineteenth century through the twentieth and continue to feel today. So through her unique narrative style and prevailing thematic concerns, Erdrich dispels notions of fixed ethnic identity and cultural history, which allows for the construction of new ways of being and being perceived in the world and offers more choice, opportunity, and liberty for the Ojibwe, despite the enduring condition of colonialism.

Colonization, Assimilation, and Cultural Identity

The central theme of colonization is rooted deeply in Erdrich's body of work. From it a number of related thematic concerns emerge, particularly the harrowing processes of assimilation and the attendant cultural identity crises faced by the Ojibwe. Much of Erdrich's literature is taken up with the struggles of full and mixed-blood Ojibwe to reconcile their Native American identity with the mainstream Euro-American culture within and around their respective Ojibwe communities. The land is the enduring symbol for Ojibwe identity, community, and survival, though it also serves as a daily reminder of colonization and what was lost. Most directly colonization is tied to the land, to place, for Erdrich. The communities of Ojibwe depicted in her fiction are centrally located in a specific geographic section of the United States—the upper northeast quadrant of North Dakota. Erdrich's birthplace, Little Falls, Minnesota; her hometown of Wahpeton, North Dakota; the Turtle Mountain Reservation in Belcourt, North Dakota; neighboring Fargo; Minneapolis–Saint Paul; the Lake Superior islands; La Pointe, Wisconsin; the Lake of the Woods area of Ontario, Canada; and various small towns along the way are all contained within the periphery. Erdrich creates a fictional world—the reservation of Little No Horse and the fictional border towns of Argus, Hoopdance, and Pluto—as an amalgam of places in the real world and has even included a map in the front matter of many of her books to approximate their location. Though cartography is usually the province of those wishing to divide communities, trace jurisdictions, define ownership, and situate power, Erdrich uses maps to illustrate the once broad expanse of Ojibwe territory, which is now reduced to neatly categorized units of officially demarcated land. The land is crisscrossed with boundaries both real and symbolic. The Ojibwe, accustomed to an ancient freedom to roam their once vast territories, an essential part of their cultural DNA, were confined to claustrophobic resettlement camps, or reservations, and their environs. The loss of land, of home, of natural resources and a centuries-old, self-sustaining independence, signaled a profound shift in Ojibwe identity and required a complete reimagining of how to be and survive in the world; it was earth-shattering. Erdrich's stress on the fundamental nature of place clearly reflects Ojibwe attitudes. A strategically well-defined sense of geographical boundaries in the New World, however, is only one of many consequences of colonization on the land depicted in Erdrich's work.

From an ecological perspective, colonization was as devastating to the natural habitat as it was to the human population, a concept Erdrich regularly explores. The Ojibwe traditionally do not live *on* the land but *with* and *for* and *because of* the land—the land is animate, a kind of sentient Mother Earth. The notion of ownership, of land deeds and treaties, was patently absurd to the Ojibwe and required a new way of thinking about the relationship between humans and nature. To be sure the Ojibwe engaged in skirmishes with neighboring tribes, particularly the Dakota Sioux, in order to ensure the reasonable distribution of land. These disputes surely were not meant to lead to the extinction of the other and often resulted in a collectively agreed upon, mutually advantageous resolution, which ensured a fair and adequate means of survival for the warring parties involved. The Ojibwe and Sioux understood the vital connection between humans and the natural world; each tribe strictly observed and respected the conservation and preservation practices of the other.

An ecocritical look at Erdrich's work points to a grave lack of environmental concern on the part of colonizing entities, revealing a genuine picture of ecological colonialism suffered at the hands of settlers and colonizers. The natural world itself was, and continues to be, colonized. The wildlife (buffalo, sturgeon, bear) and the landscape (trees, plants, wild grasses) are all impacted by colonization. Colonizing practices disrupted the natural balance and harmed the biodiversity of the land. Natural resources, once in great abundance, have become scarce due to want rather than need determining land use. A manageable and sustainable balance cannot be restored—this wound cannot heal—if the land continues to be abused. Ojibwe lands are facing a new type of colonizing threat, but one with the same goal as historical colonization: acquiring the land and its attendant economic advantages. As Erdrich explains, "Native land is under huge pressure now from the fossil fuel industry, the mining industry, the nuclear industry. In every way it can be taken, the land will be exploited or taken. If we want a future for our children and for our people we have to protect the land. And in my view, not just our land but the greater picture—the earth. After all, Native people can't disappear onto reservations when our climate begins to shift."[27] Erdrich's literary engagement with the natural world, then, is a call to action to prevent further damage and misuse of the earth to the benefit of all, not only the Ojibwe.

The advent of Euro-American settlement necessitated a new manner of being in the world. Ojibwe tribal values, attitudes, and means of existence, so inextricably linked with the land, the seasons, the weather, and natural resources, required a radical ontological and epistemological revisioning in order to survive the onslaught of colonization. Ultimately the Ojibwe had to choose whether to hang back and fight in order to save their heritage against insurmountable odds or to assimilate and trust in the ancient perseverance of their aboriginal tribe. Erdrich's dramatization of these negotiations, based on a mix of oral tradition, personal testimony, family history, documentary historical evidence, and intuitive imagination, is a hallmark of her literature. Through institutionalized religious, educational, economic, and political means, the colonizers employed a campaign of assimilation, humiliation, shame, and racism to facilitate the acculturation of generations of Ojibwe. In more subtle ways, mission churches scattered throughout Native American territories, English-language schools, and intermarriage or cohabitation contributed to the pressure on Ojibwe to become a part of a seemingly innocuous foreign community, a new "tribe" interested in sharing the land. By conflating the ideas of whiteness and piety, the Western world employed Christianity in many subversive ways, resulting in many Ojibwe experiencing shame and cultural dislocation. Erdrich offers a procession of full and half-blooded Ojibwe characters who testify to those who suffered humiliation, confusion, and psychological, emotional, and spiritual fragmentation trying to balance on a cultural hinge between two diametrically opposed worlds. This cultural identity crisis, often framed in terms of religious fanaticism, historical trauma, familial dysfunction, political strife, economic hardship, and psychological instability, represents a very real part of Ojibwe existence during the time of colonization and persists well into the twenty-first century.

In many of Erdrich's texts, dislocation and isolation from the community is evident. Many Ojibwe ultimately distanced themselves from their Native roots and embraced a decidedly Western way of being. Where many elders remain elegiac and reverent when describing the terrific loss suffered by their people, the younger generation has found interests outside of the community, in the world at large. Instead of putting emphasis on the "we" of the clan, their focus is on "I," the individual apart from the community, in characteristic "each man for himself" Western, capitalist fashion. This privileging of the self—this self-centeredness—is in direct opposition to the traditional Ojibwe idea of communal living. Part of this emotional and cultural retreat from Ojibwe values resulted initially from Catholic mission schools and then from the Indian boarding school experience of many Ojibwe children, an assimilation practice adopted by the U.S. government with the goal of deracination in the late nineteenth and early twentieth centuries. The emotional, spiritual, and cultural toll on these children, their progeny, and the generations to follow is a key concern in many of Erdrich's texts.

The education provided in the boarding school system created disparate, often competing allegiances in Ojibwe children. The students, who were forbidden to speak in Native languages, perform indigenous spiritual ceremonies, follow Native customs, or dress in traditional clothing, utterly relied on their Euro-American caretakers, complete strangers whose language and customs were largely foreign to them. The children were compelled to accept the boarding school conditions, not by choice but in order to survive—where else could they turn for food, shelter, and clothing so far from home or the reservation? In terms of the education provided, patriotism was the prevailing goal of the boarding-school curriculum rather than preparation for successful lives in a discipline of the students' choosing. Erdrich explained that "much of patriotic culture is also based on the fact that boarding schools were run by the U.S. government, and so included pledges of allegiance, flags, lots of patriotic propaganda, and patriotic pageantry in the curriculum."[28] Tied up with the boarding school system was the U.S. military, which might account for the number of veterans in Erdrich's writing.

Patriotism for the Ojibwe is obviously problematic, as it would seem at odds with tribal nationalism or the fight for sovereignty. Many of the Ojibwe children of the mid-twentieth century were the product of boarding-school-educated parents and grandparents, whose alliances and loyalties were split between two worlds—Native American and the United States. In this way many younger generations of Ojibwe feel an authentic connection to both cultures. Erdrich notes that "the American Flag comes out first with Tribal Flags and the Eagle Staffs in powwows. War Veterans carry the flags and are always honored."[29] Of course the central question remains: why would the Ojibwe trust that the U.S. government would treat Native American soldiers any better than Native American civilians? With so many damaged and neglected Anishinaabeg veterans, choosing military service seems ironic and tragic. Yet Native Americans continue to fight for the United States, as Erdrich portrays in the characters of Henry Lamartine Jr. in *Love Medicine* and Morris in *The Painted Drum,* two examples of the tragedy of fighting in U.S. wars. On one level the high rate of enlistment among Native Americans is a matter of patriotism; on another it is an economic issue, as it is for many Americans who join up at age eighteen because they have no other prospects. Erdrich explains the tendrils of connection binding patriotism, military service, economics, and the boarding school system:

> Native Americans have always enlisted in great numbers for a very small statistical population. My relatives have served in all branches of the American military. The reasons for this particular form of patriotism are complicated. First and foremost, I think, is the opportunity the military has always presented in terms of training and economic incentives. Unfortunately, it is one of the few options for people in a country where higher education is not subsidized. But historically it is more than that. Many children attended military boarding schools, or boarding schools run on a military model from the late nineteenth century to the 1930's when some of the regulations were relaxed. . . . Native people were trained into the military—many reported that going into the military felt comfortable. They had been living with bells and discipline all of their lives.[30]

Eventually the Ojibwe took back a measure of control in the general education of their children, which stimulated a growing interest in Ojibwe youth to learn about a lost cultural heritage and provided an opportunity for tribal communities to restore and reinforce Ojibwe values. Erdrich explained that "now tribal cultures are finding ways to resurrect their own histories and philosophies in teaching their children."[31] In fact the frame tale in Erdrich's *Tracks,* the occasion for telling the story, is the narrator Nanapush's effort to reacculturate Lulu Nanapush, his adopted granddaughter, on her return from boarding school by sharing the history of the community, in which her mother, Fleur Pillager, figures prominently. Connection becomes the overwhelming message of Nanapush's tale and, more generally, of the Ojibwe historical narrative, as evidenced in Erdrich's oeuvre. Erdrich regularly creates various and complex ties of kinship and family history in her fiction. Kinship takes on particular significance and urgency in the reservation world. In the insular communities of Ojibwe, the unity of the inhabitants, in the face of ever-encroaching U.S. government policies and culture, is vital to the tribe's proliferation and success. Many of Erdrich's texts include genealogical charts illustrating the complex connections between and among several families; the family names Nanapush, Pillager, Kashpaw, Morrissey, Lazarre, Lamartine, and Shaawano commonly appear, cross, and divide in these charts. In terms of narrative intrigue, the charts also expose long-buried historical connections and shocking family revelations. The same families persist from story to story, novel to novel. The reason for these elaborate genealogical charts is not only to prove the inherent connectedness of the community but also to serve as evidence of the perseverance of the Ojibwe.

Finally storytelling is the means by which Ojibwe cultural heritage and history is communicated in Erdrich's writing. Traditionally the history of the tribe, its customs and behaviors, ceremonies and beliefs, were passed down through storytelling. The history of colonization and its effect on the Ojibwe was passed down through oral tradition as well. Storytelling is the means by which Ojibwe history is remembered and preserved and an integral cultural component of Ojibwe identity. Erdrich has explained that "memory is all. Memory is where the language resided, because it was an oral language. The stories were not written down."[32] From Nanapush and Father Damien to Mooshum and Joe Coutts, the multitude of Erdrich's storytellers function as documentarians of time and place, in and around the reservation. With humor and pathos, in the face of adversity if not extinction, these storytellers—poets, prophets, tricksters, teachers, sinners, and saints—are on the continuum between loss and recovery, both personally and culturally. Like so many of her characters, Erdrich will not be deterred in her singular purpose of bearing witness to the trials and tragedies, the victories and accomplishments, and the recovery, perseverance, and survival of the Ojibwe people.

CHAPTER 2

Love Medicine, The Bingo Palace, and *The Painted Drum*

Louise Erdrich's first novel, *Love Medicine* (1984), catapulted her to the front of what Kenneth Lincoln describes as the "Native American Renaissance," wherein Native American authors "are writing prolifically, particularly the women, who correlate feminist, nativist, and artistic commitments in a compelling rebirth."[1] Lincoln not only placed Erdrich as a rising star among Native American authors but also suggested that she stands alongside the greats of American letters: "Louise Erdrich may belong with O'Connor, Fitzgerald, Hemingway, and Welty. It is not often, indeed seldom, that a writer word for word, character by character, action to action, story following story, surprises, upsets, terrifies, delights, saddens, and amazes a reader—this one does."[2] Lincoln's appraisal is just one of the many positive reactions that the novel garnered upon its publication. Accordingly the preponderance of Erdrich scholarship is devoted to *Love Medicine,* analyzing the novel's characters, themes, symbols, and style, applying various critical lenses from postmodernism to feminism, and arguing for its place in the study of American literature.

Love Medicine is the beginning of an epic, a series of novels detailing the historical and contemporary effects of colonialism on various clans of Ojibwe from Minnesota and North Dakota. Erdrich explains in an author's note appended to a 2009 edition of the novel that "since writing *Love Medicine,* I have understood that I am writing one long book in which the main chapters are also books titled *Tracks, Four Souls, The Bingo Palace, The Last Report on the Miracles at Little No Horse,* and *The Painted Drum.*"[3] Each book in the series adds an essential piece of the puzzle, creating a complex picture of the lives of her numerous, interconnected characters, a diversity that echoes her use of multiple narrators within those novels. While each book stands alone, and chapters of many of them have been excerpted as short stories, taken together the books in the series offer an insight to the vast scope and depth of the community Erdrich has created, rivaling William Faulkner's Yoknapatawpha County in American letters.

Parsing these novels into two groups provides for a more manageable discussion of the epic series. They can be reasonably divided into the contemporary, *Love Medicine, The Bingo Palace,* and *The Painted Drum,* and the historical, *Tracks, Four Souls,* and *The Last Report on the Miracles at Little No Horse.* Though none of Erdrich's novels can be described as exclusively historical or contemporary, since interweaving the past and present is a hallmark of her writing, dividing them into these two categories is a useful method by which readers of Erdrich can follow certain narrative and thematic threads as opposed to considering them chronologically by publication date. The contemporary novels discussed in this chapter follow *Love Medicine* chronologically and feature the theme of assimilation, which unfolds by degrees over the course of the novels. The historical novels, taken up in the following chapter, predate much of the time period *Love Medicine* spans narratively and offer an indispensable history of various characters encountered in the contemporary novels.

No comprehensive discussion of Erdrich's fictional oeuvre can proceed without some discussion of *Love Medicine,* which introduced readers to Erdrich's distinctive narrative style, along with a number of characters, families, and themes that have featured in most of her subsequent novels. Whether tangentially or directly, *Love Medicine* casts a wide net over her fictional town of Argus, the reservation towns of Little No Horse and Hoopdance, and the cities of Fargo and Minneapolis–Saint Paul, commonly referred to as "the Cities." Through its short story–like, episodic chapters, the novel spans nearly six decades, from the 1930s to the 1980s. *Love Medicine,* which Erdrich revised and expanded in 1995 and again in 2005, follows the lives of five interconnected families: primarily the Kashpaws, Lamartines, and Morrisseys and peripherally the Pillagers and the Lazarres. The thematic concerns of the novel are many: storytelling and oral tradition, kinship and community, Catholicism and Ojibwe spirituality, Western culture and Ojibwe tradition, the written word and spoken language, boundaries and limits, real and symbolic wars, and particularly identity and its formation and fragmentation.

Marie Kashpaw is a mixed-blood Ojibwe character, embodying many of the themes of the novel and the many cultural trials suffered by the Ojibwe, particularly in terms of the resulting identity crisis caused by forced assimilation. Her marriage to Nector Kashpaw, son of Margaret Kashpaw (Rushes Bear), life on the reservation, interactions with the other main characters, and her tangled history with the many clans fuel much of the plot and themes of the book. In the chapter "St Marie," set in the mid-1930s, Erdrich presents readers with a haunting and memorable scene involving the violent yoking of Western religious values and Ojibwe cultural traditions embodied in Marie's character. Erdrich relates her encounter with Sister Leopolda, an overzealous nun in the local Sacred Heart convent, who becomes a central character in the historical novels of the series. Readers receive a glimpse at the depth of Marie's identity crisis and spiritual fracture as Sister Leopolda takes her under her sinister wing as a protégée. Marie is proud to be as light-skinned as the nuns at the convent and insists that this lets her "pray as good as they could," since she does not have "that much Indian blood" (43). Unimpressed, Sister Leopolda consistently reprimands Marie for being "Indian" and subjects her to a spiritual purging that is actually physical abuse and arguably torture. Sister Leopolda alternately kicks Marie, pours boiling water from a kettle onto her back, and finally stabs her through the hand with a burning iron poker. As a result of her abuse, Marie becomes obsessed with becoming a saint and having the nuns worship at her feet, akin to Sister Leopolda's own fanatical religious views and sense of superiority. The superiority they both yearn for, however, is borne out of a deep insecurity and fear. Marie likens herself to "those bush Indians who stole the holy black hat of a Jesuit and swallowed little scraps of it to cure their fevers. But the hat itself carried smallpox and was killing them with belief" (45). Somewhere in her psyche, Marie believes she deserves this physical punishment, which is the way the Ojibwe must commune with the Catholic God. Erdrich is clearly alerting the reader to the ways in which spiritual colonization not only inflicted emotional damage but also had real, physical effects.

Moving forward into the 1970s, Erdrich presents a more contemporary view of the price of colonization. She portrays a part of Native American life rarely discussed in mainstream American history—the service of Native Americans in the U.S. military. Using this as the background for another example of the tenuous relationship between the Ojibwe and the general U.S. population, Erdrich depicts the precarious marginal identity of Ojibwe serviceman Henry Lamartine Jr. and his identification as a U.S. citizen for the purposes of war. In the chapters "A Bridge" and "The Red Convertible," Erdrich dramatizes the irony of a man fighting in a war for a country that does not recognize the sovereignty of his people. Henry, one of Lulu Lamartine's sons, serves as a marine in Vietnam and becomes a POW for roughly six months (167). He survives but returns mentally and emotionally broken. As health care was generally hard won on the reservation, mental health treatment for post-traumatic stress disorder would have been nonexistent. Henry is "routinely questioned by a military psychiatrist" upon his return and then simply "dismissed" (167). Once he is home, there are “no Indian doctors on the reservation” (182) who can offer follow-up treatment in a culturally sensitive way. He “carried enough shrapnel deep inside of him, still working its way out, to set off the metal detector in the airport” upon his return to the States (167). While the “whole war was solved in the government’s mind,” it will “keep on going” in Henry’s mind (182).

Henry’s role as a soldier in Vietnam is distinctive because he is a Native American. In essence he is fighting for the country that stole the land of his people and continues to subvert their fundamental rights. Erdrich considers Henry to be unexceptional in this regard: “I know plenty of Native people who served proudly in wars and to whom the world opened up, who recall those years fondly. Also there are the fathers and mothers lost forever in foreign countries fighting wars that have never made a difference for Native people.”[4] Like thousands of other Native Americans, Henry wants to help defend the land of his ancestors and goes off to war in a foreign country. During the Vietnam War, the United States itself was not threatened, of course, but Native American soldiers were still compelled by an ironic, if not troubling, patriotism that stemmed from their sacred connection to the land and also the sworn duty to protect it.

Henry failed to anticipate a horror of war particular to his cultural perspective: he finds himself identifying with the Vietnamese in the heat of battle. He recalls a painful episode from his service when a superior officer ordered him to question a Vietnamese woman, ostensibly a Vietcong, who had been bayonetted and lay dying. The woman begged Henry for mercy, saying, “You, me, same. Same.” She pointed “to her eyes and his eyes. The Asian, folded eyes of some Chippewas” (172). That identification haunts Henry, who identified with the fellow nonwhite person in this dire situation. Soldiers of the same U.S. government slaughtered his own people during the Indian Wars and after. Here Erdrich confronts the reader with an aspect of Native American life neglected in the annals of U.S. wars, while also providing another facet of the struggle for Native Americans to be at one with their heritage and with their contemporary existence.

Arriving at the 1980s, Erdrich presents a contemporary example of what is lost through assimilation; the remnants of colonialism persist in present-day Ojibwe life. When Lipsha Morrissey is asked by his adoptive grandmother, the elderly Marie Kashpaw, to prepare a “love medicine” to win back the affections of her husband, Nector, whose laser focus is on Lulu Lamartine, Lipsha’s biological grandmother, hilarity and tragedy ensue. Erdrich’s use of the word *medicine* is not in the Western pharmaceutical sense but describes a combination of traditional poultices, herbal tinctures, spiritual healing practices, sweat lodges, and vision quests. Together with *love,* which connotes passion, sex, spirituality, connection, and kinship, it is a powerful tool and healing art that soothes everything from lost passion in a marriage to existential and spiritual despair. Lipsha is aware of the traditional Ojibwe meaning of "love medicine" and the method of preparation but opts for a new way, a shortcut. Substituting convenience store replacements for various traditional items, Lipsha decides a turkey heart from a frozen supermarket bird is as good as a goose heart from a living bird he has hunted and killed for the occasion (242). Nector pays the ultimate price for Lipsha's disregard for the old ways; he chokes on the turkey heart and dies. Lipsha's assimilation causes great upheaval in the family, as well as the death of a beloved character.

These are just a few instances in the novel of Erdrich's attention to the contemporary crises Ojibwe face. Storytelling, for Erdrich, is a type of love medicine; it has the power to heal ancient wounds and to preserve culture. *Love Medicine* is the beginning of a long story of a community and a people that is continued in five more novels. In fact Lipsha's story continues in *The Bingo Palace,* which further considers the ways he has assimilated to his detriment and his struggles with his cultural identity.

The Bingo Palace

In *The Bingo Palace* (1994), Erdrich picks up several of the narrative threads introduced in *Love Medicine.* Though published a decade later, it is the direct sequel to that earlier novel. In terms of narrative form and thematic concerns, Erdrich maintains her multiple-narrator style and commitment to dramatizing the enduring effects of colonization: the consequences of assimilation, the struggle to create a stable cultural identity or negotiate a tenable balance between two conflicting cultures, and the necessary recognition and reconciliation required to come to terms with all that has been lost for the Ojibwe. In terms of narrative style, the novel alternates between first-person and third-person narration. Some chapters are narrated by Lipsha Morrissey or by a communal *we,* while all of the other accounts of the remaining characters in the novel are in third person. The communal narrators act much like a Greek chorus, training their judgmental and discriminating eyes on the events of the community. In the first chapter, this *we,* embodying the spirit of the community, introduces the novel, with an empathetic nod to the reader: "Some of us tried to resist, yet were pulled in just the same. We were curious to know more, even though we'd never grasp the whole of it. The story comes around, pushing at our brains, and soon we are trying to ravel back to the beginning, trying to put families into order and make sense of things. But we start with one person, and soon another and another follows, and still another, until we are lost in the connections."[5] Like the reader the people of the community feel compelled by Erdrich's story and yet are confounded by the complex relations among the various family members, the complications of kinship and family ties. Within the community there is a prurient desire to watch the doings and undoings of the characters, in hopes of creating more salacious tales and gossip—a seemingly popular, low-level type of storytelling among the Ojibwe, as it is with most collectives of creative, social human beings. Speculation and sensationalism characterize much of the talk surrounding the reservation. This apparently casual talk is actually an integral part of the oral tradition of the Ojibwe. It is through storytelling that lives are not forgotten, memories are passed down through the generations, and history is written; the cultural trauma of dispossession is healed in part through storytelling.

In *The Bingo Palace* the communal voice comments on many of the major players in *Love Medicine* and continues their stories: Lulu Lamartine is busy running the tribe; convicted murderer Gerry Nanapush, with his Nanapush eyes, "Pillager bones", "shy rage", "serious wonder", and great head of hair, remains a ne'er-do-well (4); Lyman Lamartine is a "dark-minded schemer," "a bitter and yet shaman-pleasant entrepreneur" who has "his own interests so mingled with his people's that he couldn't tell his personal ambition from the pride of the Kashpaws" (5); Albertine Johnson is busy alternately dancing in powwows or poring over her textbooks from the medical library; Fleur, "always a half-spirit anyway," still stays in her woods, with one foot on death road, though the community wishes she would "settle her bones in the sun with us and take rest, instead of wasting her last words on that medicine boy [Lipsha]" (6); and "June Morrissey still walks through that sudden Easter snow" (5). The harshest communal assessment is of Lipsha, who does not appreciate his "powers," which were "weakened and confused" by going back and forth from the reservation to the city of Fargo (7). The community "[doesn't] know him and [doesn't] want to and [doesn't] care" (9). Lipsha's perceived abandonment of Ojibwe cultural heritage is the greatest indictment against him and situates him as an outlier, a poseur, and a symbol of surrender—of easy assimilation. What the community initially overlooks is Lipsha's sincere and earnest attempt to find a place where he authentically belongs, a place to call home.

When Lipsha returned to the reservation permanently and attended a winter intertribal ceremony, onlookers recall, "he slid through the crowd during the middle of an intertribal song. We saw him edge against the wall to watch the whirling bright dancers, and immediately we had to notice that there was no place the boy could fit" (9). The narrative then shifts in the second chapter to Lipsha's first-person account of events. His self-awareness is keen: "I am all at once confused and shy-faced and back where I belong without a place to fit, a person to turn to, a friend to greet" (11). The shifting narrative voice is consistent with Erdrich's narrative style in almost all of her novels and signals a change in perspective, giving a more fully developed picture of events. The first-person eyewitness accounts are literally "I witness" accounts, fully contestable and subjective personal interpretations of events. The loss of Ojibwe culture and language are embodied in Lipsha's first-person narrative. The mixing of traditions and popular culture results in an identity crisis. Lipsha identifies with his Ojibwe roots, but he also immerses himself in popular Western culture. He feels at home on the reservation but finds life more interesting among non-Indians in the cities. Much to his confusion and chagrin, neither culture welcomes him with open arms. Lipsha struggles to fit in and survive in these dual worlds.

Lipsha throws in his lot with the ever-entrepreneurial Lyman Lamartine, who following the disastrous end to his tomahawk factory, detailed in *Love Medicine,* finds a new interest in gambling, venturing to increase his economic and social standing through bingo halls and casinos. The main focus of Lipsha's narrative throughout the novel, however, is his romantic obsession with Shawnee Ray, who is engaged to Lyman, his own kin and employer, and the lengths he will go to win her heart. Erdrich also grows her complex family tree in *The Bingo Palace,* presenting Lipsha as the embodiment of the various branches and bloodlines: he was adopted as a grandson by Marie Lazarre and Nector Kashpaw but is the son of Gerry Nanapush and June Morrissey, whose death is described in the beginning of *Love Medicine.* Lyman is the result of an extramarital affair, the illegitimate son of Lipsha's grandmother Lulu and Nector. As Lipsha explains, "The truth is, our relationship is complicated by some factors over which we have no control. His real father was my stepfather. His mother is my grandmother. His half brother is my father. I have an instant crush upon his girl" (16). The historical intermingling dooms Lipsha to have a romantic interest in Lyman's girlfriend, as in the plays of the "old time Greeks" (17). It comes as no surprise to Lipsha that he would enmesh himself in an even more complicated relationship with Lyman: "It is natural for us Indians, we're so used to inner plot twists that we just laugh. . . . From day one, we're loaded down. History, personal politics, tangled bloodlines" (17). The intricacies of shared genealogy among Erdrich's characters do not lead to disorientation and an unstable identity. On the contrary the complex systems of kinship instead establish connection, community, and lasting relationships.

While basking in the shade of his family tree, Lipsha's real confusion stems from his efforts at balancing his Western and Ojibwe identities. He possesses an abiding belief that material things will ensure happiness. During much of the novel, he tirelessly plays bingo to win the grand prize, the bingo van, which he believes will win Shawnee Ray's heart. He does finally win the van but learns that the value of material things is ephemeral and can herald a person's downfall. In an episode at a 7-Eleven convenience store, Lipsha engages in a verbal sparring match with a clerk from Montana named Marty, who calls Lipsha a "Prairie Nigger" under his breath. Later Marty and some of his friends attack Lipsha and commandeer his van. Lipsha makes small talk to delay the inevitable thrashing, inquiring from which states the men came to North Dakota. When they tell him Kansas and South Dakota, Lipsha reflects on the shapes of those states and arrives at a troubling conclusion: "It isn't that I really have a thing against those places, understand, it's just that the straight-edged shape is not a Chippewa preference. You look around, and everything you see is round, everything in nature. There are no perfect boundaries, no natural borders except winding rivers. Only human-made things tend toward cubes and squares, the van, for instance. That is an example. Suddenly I realized that I am driving a four-wheeled version of the state of North Dakota" (81). In this moment Lipsha begins to reconsider his strategy and the value of his prized North Dakota–shaped bingo van. He realizes his fantasy of winning Shawnee Ray by seducing her with material possessions is misguided.

Trying a different kind of tack, since his materialism gets him nowhere with Shawnee Ray, Lipsha seeks the counsel of his great-grandmother Fleur Pillager to learn the old, traditional ways of Ojibwe "love medicine." One day he follows Fleur to their ancestral land, on Matchimanito Lake, the land where his father, Gerry, was probably conceived and possibly also his grandmother Lulu. Of course Lipsha remembers the disastrous attempt, recounted in *Love Medicine,* to create a love medicine for his adoptive grandparents, Marie and Nector, when he "tried to doctor his grandfather with the store-bought love medicine that ended up so tragic and confused" (124). But he recognizes that by blood rights, Fleur is his great-grandmother, "the one who started it all in motion" (125), and he feels semiconfident she will help him get it right this time around. With equal parts fear and respect, he follows her to her cabin in the bush. While "she must be a hundred years old," Fleur's speed and strength during the hike in the woods leaves Lipsha thinking she must "only be more like ninety, at most" (132). On the way he is shocked by the land they traverse: "I knew the reservation inside and out, I thought, but it turns out I knew it by car, not by foot" (133). The artificial boundaries drawn and paved into the streets of the town limit the perspective of Lipsha and those of his generation. In Fleur's time the travel through the reservation was by foot, a direct connection with the land, not by impersonal mechanical or technological means and certainly not by a bingo van. The Ojibwe lived a fairly peripatetic existence, traveling to different areas seasonally in their boundless territories.

Upon reaching Fleur's cabin, Lipsha notes the pristine landscape surrounding it and the condition inside the dwelling. Much like the apartment in the senior community in town where her daughter Lulu lives, Fleur's traditional cabin is flooded with the detritus of history: papers, folders, files, newspapers, more files, and clippings. Lipsha notices "the hairline cracks and patterns of tangles, thread lines on the whitewashed walls" (134). These lines, he soon realizes, are sentences and words, Fleur's personal documentation of events on the reservation, her own historical record. Both his grandmother and great-grandmother have a real commitment to preserving the history of the clan for later generations. Lulu is publicly and politically focused, "collecting papers and Congressional records and magazines" (128) and seeking "to reclaim the original reservation, no less" (129). Fleur's dispossession and reclamation of her ancestral land, which is the subject of a number of Erdrich's novels, allows her a more private and resigned look at history. The fight for Ojibwe land is now Lulu's mission, but a record of the land and its people and of her own momentous revenge will surely benefit the younger generation.

The circumstance by which Fleur reclaims her land is a game of chance. Like her great-grandson, who has a flair for bingo, Fleur puts all of her hopes in a card game to secure the deed to the land she lost to a lumber baron, circumstances that are fully explored in the novel *Four Souls*. Her return to the reservation after these events is described in terms much like Lipsha's return. The first-person plural, the voice of the community, is also used: "Everyone knew and did not know her. There were no cries of greeting, no hands held admiringly to the face and smiles. No one smoothed Fleur's hair down on each side of her forehead and said 'Daughter, daughter, we've missed you. Peendigaen. Sit and eat some of this good soup.' No one offered her bread and tea. Only sharp-eyed gossipers already hurried to build story onto story" (139–40). They note her countenance as a woman who carried herself "always as though she owned everything and nothing: sky, earth, those who crossed her path, road, and Pillager land. It was because she owned herself, they said, because she was a four-souled woman. Like her grandmother, Fleur Pillager possessed more souls than she had a right to." Erdrich makes this concept the basis of *Four Souls*, published nearly a decade after *The Bingo Palace*. Here readers encounter the crumbs of what become the full-blown stories of the historical novels in the Love Medicine series.

Lipsha does earn insight and medicine from Fleur, and he also inherits the Pillager name, which facilitates his construction of a stable identity. Fleur insists that he use *Pillager* rather than *Morrissey* with its negative associations. The goal of keeping the family name alive fell to her many decades before and now "there's none of us left," so Lipsha must carry on the name. Lipsha's identity crisis thus eases in a spiritual and emotional sense, but he is still waiting for proof positive self-identification, "a complicated thing in Indian Country" (128). Because of land allotments by the U.S. government, members of the tribe had to prove bloodlines for inheritance or subsidies. Lipsha is waiting for a band card, "trying out of boredom to prove who I am—the useless son of a criminal father and a mother who dies with her hands full of snow. . . . I don't have my enrollment and entitlements stabilized, not yet, nor do I have my future figured exactly out" (128). The conflict that arises from this position is faced by many of the younger generation of Ojibwe and other Native American tribes and carries with it insecurity about roots, origins, and self. Though Lipsha's identity is unstable and in flux, his visit with Fleur provides a necessary foundation.

Religion is also a theme in the novel, with Lipsha expressing his views on Catholicism and traditional Ojibwe beliefs. He cannot conceive of Catholic Communion, as it is "eating the real true and precious body and the blood of Christ," and yet "the Catholics make such a big deal out of converting cannibals? Drinking blood, eating flesh, it goes on at every mass" (157). The idea of confession also irks him: "saying a few Hail Marys or some Our Fathers lets sinners off scot-free" (157), with no restitution demanded and no community service, which does not comport with his way of thinking or with Ojibwe ideas of justice and penance. After visiting with his great-grandmother Fleur at her cabin, he learns that he does have a nascent interest in Ojibwe spirituality. Lipsha has no illusions that the Ojibwe religion is any better than Catholicism, but it may help prove to Shawnee Ray that he has staying power. His main motivation in adopting traditional beliefs is impressing her.

To this end he tries out different rituals, including accompanying Lyman on a vision quest on Xavier Toose's land, at the edge of an allotment that blends into Fleur Pillager's land around Matchimanito Lake (191). Toose is a medicine man who lives a traditional Ojibwe life. He is also Shawnee Ray's uncle, which is even more motivation for Lipsha to embark on the vision quest. He has had visions in the past: when he was cracked on the head by an old vet with a wine bottle (160), which was an accident but convinced Lipsha to join the army, for example, and when he interacts with his deceased mother, June, whose spirit seems to be alive and well, a real presence in the community. The vision quest is more than he bargains for, though, as it is by the book and traditional: "Things are moving quicker than I hope, maybe even than I wanted. I had in mind something less radical than four or maybe six days alone in the bush with no food" (159). Immediately Xavier instructs Lipsha to help with the construction of a sweat lodge, which will be the first step in the ceremony. Gathering, stripping, and shaping birch branches and twigs, the men construct the lodge and fill it with the heated stones that will let off steam as medicine and water are poured over them. Lipsha's questions during the process and once in the sweat lodge reveal his unfamiliarity with traditional beliefs and his deep-rooted connection to his American values. He confesses that "a banana split would taste good" (192), compares the opening prayers to the opening lecture at a conference, and notes "the Terminator-muscled convict type with a lot of tattoos" manning the hot stones (192–93).

Once he is released and sent into the woods for his vision quest, Lipsha, feeling like a "cooked steak" (194), proceeds to have a fitful night of sleep, conjuring wild beasts in his vicinity waiting to tear him limb from limb—"Fangs, tusks, rabbit incisors. Jaws for tearing. Sharks. Forget Sharks. Bears. Raccoons. In this overbearing dark, I won't see it coming. Slashing death" (196)—though such threats are improbable in the serene woodland location where he camps. On the first morning, due to his hunger, Lipsha's visions consist of Big Macs (196). He continues his vision quest, while wishing for books to read, movies to watch, or his Walkman: "I rewatch all the *Godfather* series, then reread the *Dune* trilogy and my Kashpaw dad's favorite *Moby Dick*" (198), which is appropriate, as his major vision is proving as elusive as Herman Melville's great white whale. He thinks of the hot dog he did not eat at the Dairy Queen, with its mustard and sweet relish, which leads him to imagine the lightly salty sweat on Shawnee's neck. Western materialism and Ojibwe spirituality are mixed in his visions, symbolizing the struggle between his assimilated and traditional ways of knowing and being.

Ultimately Lipsha achieves a major vision in the form of a skunk. The skunk's grand pronouncement is "This ain't real estate" (200). The land Lipsha camps on, his ancestral Pillager land, is slated to be used for the titular "bingo palace" that Lyman wants to build with the help of Lipsha's bingo winnings. His connection with his ancestors is strong, as is evidenced in this vision. The others in the group, including Lyman, find this hilarious, focusing on the messenger, the skunk, instead of its message. All animals have their symbolic purpose for the Ojibwe, and Lipsha recognizes that "the skunk is right, for the complex is slated to develop Pillager land, partly Fleur's land and partly old allotments that the tribe holds in common, and which is fractionated through the dead and scattered holdouts who have never signed the treaties that gave away so much of what we called ours" (219). The skunk shows Lipsha a vision of the future, in which the casino brings irrevocable change and the loss of his ancestral land: "Where Fleur's cabin stands, a parking lot will be rolled out of asphalt. Over Pillager grave markers, sawed by wind and softened, blackjack tables. Where the trees that shelter brown birds rise, bright banks of slot machines. Out upon the lake that the lion man inhabits, where Pillagers drowned and lived, where black stones still roll round to the surface, the great gaming room will face with picture windows" (219). Time reveals that the vision is true, and all of the skunk's warnings come to pass as Lyman continues his land development project on Pillager land. Lipsha notes that "it's not completely one way or another, traditional against the bingo. You have to stay alive to keep your tradition alive and working," but "everybody knows bingo money is not based on solid ground" (221). Money has "no substance, there's nothing left when the day is done but a pack of receipts. . . . Our reservation is not real estate, luck fades when sold. . . . Attraction has no staying power, no weight, no heart" (221). Though armed with this knowledge and a sense of what is right for his people, Lipsha does not stand in the way of the bingo palace, and another piece of land, another piece of the Ojibwe, is forever lost to commerce.

In addition to Ojibwe real estate, Erdrich describes another casualty to assimilation—the Ojibwe language. Though brimming with Erdrich's characteristic humor, one of the most poignant scenes in the novel is when "Gerry No-shit-barn-built-can-hold-a-Chippewa Nanapush" escapes jail once again and calls Lipsha, his son, to come to his aid. Afraid that the phone call could be overheard or traced, Gerry uses the old language, Ojibwe, to communicate his whereabouts to his son. Unfortunately Lipsha remembers only bits and pieces of Ojibwe and guesses at the meaning: "My father is either playing Star Wars games at Arts Arcade, or he is holed up at the Fargo library, or he is hiding curled up in the lodge dumpster of the Sons of Norway" (223). Lipsha admits that his intrinsic understanding of the Ojibwe he discovered the day he spent at Fleur's was only an anomaly inspired by his fear of his great-grandmother: "I don't know our traditional language all that well. Now the lack catches up with me. To my horror, I'm not sure what my father revealed to me on the phone. I work out each word with a pencil, then erase it. I fix on each syllable, slippery as a minnow. In the end, however, all I can make out are these three strange possibilities. It occurs to me, though, that I'd better get to Fargo before the library closes tomorrow or before Dad runs out of quarters or before the day of civic garbage pickup" (233). This deficiency shifts events irrevocably in the story. Had Lipsha understood his father, he would have met him at the Sons of Norway lodge. Instead he spends time at a video arcade and a library before finally finding the dumpster at the lodge. The comedy of Lipsha's character, his endearing goofiness, is evident in his absurd notion that Gerry would be playing video games. Perhaps he innocently imagines his father has assimilated in the same ways as he has. Erdrich creates a deep pathos in the scene and a real sense of the loss of language through the generations of the colonized Ojibwe. All of the Western cultural trappings, represented by video-game technology and the written word in the library, again supplant the best-laid schemes of the Ojibwe.

Not only is the language lost in *The Bingo Palace,* but Fleur's ultimate sacrifice, death, is also depicted at the novel's end. She realizes that Lipsha, one of the last remaining heirs of the Pillagers, is caught out in the long, disruptive blizzard, and "annoyed, she took his place" (272). She trades places with him on the death road, so that he can survive the episode in which he helps his father escape the authorities in a stolen car. She recognizes Lipsha's importance in the survival of her bloodline, in continuing the story, and so offers up her own soul to spare her great-grandson's life. Though Lipsha's story lacks a definitive end in *The Bingo Palace,* the important themes his story represents—the harms of assimilation, the struggle for identity, and the strength of kinship—continue to be thematic concerns in the rest of the Love Medicine series.

The Painted Drum

While *The Painted Drum* (2005) is geographically removed from the other novels of the Love Medicine series, it shares many thematic concerns: assimilation, deracination, kinship, dispossession, identity construction, and Ojibwe cultural survival. In a departure for Erdrich, the setting is New England, with a central return to the fictional reservation north of Hoopdance in North Dakota during the course of the novel. The novel's setting symbolizes the colonial effects still felt in the contemporary life of displaced Ojibwe and their progeny as it shifts from the present in New England to the reservation in North Dakota and back again. It is divided into four parts: the first and last parts, narrated by Faye Travers in New Hampshire, frame the rest of the narrative, while the second part (narrated by Bernard Shaawano) and third part (narrated in the third person) are both set on the reservation in North Dakota. The narrative progression echoes the main characters' literal and symbolic journeys and that of the novel's central symbol, the painted drum.

The story of the novel is largely driven by the story of the painted drum: its creation, history, purpose, and its displacement and return home to the reservation. *The Painted Drum* is also a human story of connection, redemption, and healing. While Erdrich has characters in other works that have assimilated, mostly in terms of religion, the Travers women are the most isolated from the reservation, both physically and culturally; they are part of the Ojibwe diaspora. The assimilation that has diluted many Ojibwe and mixed-blood descendants is evident in the characters of Faye, an estate sales dealer specializing in Native American artifacts, and her mother, Elsie Travers, living in a small New Hampshire town called Stiles and Stokes. Faye has only a superficial, secondhand understanding of her Ojibwe bloodlines and vaguely acknowledges that her maternal grandmother was originally from a reservation in North Dakota. Elsie herself is "perfectly assimilated, cold-blooded and analytical about the reservation present, and utterly dismissive of history."[6] Faye's father and sister Netta are deceased, leaving the women on their own.

The Travers women lack community and live solitary lives, with no personal connections other than with those who live in their immediate neighborhood, notably Kurt Krahe, a German American artist who is Faye's lover, and the strange and reclusive Kit Tatro, who is obsessed with discovering seemingly nonexistent Native American roots in his bloodline. Even those connections are tenuous; Kurt wonders why Faye is offended by his nickname for Kit, "Squaw Man Tatro," and she has to explain that it is "an insult to us," pointing at her mother (55). Kurt is oblivious to her cultural heritage or simply dismissive of it and is more deeply embroiled in his personal suffering and artistic struggles. Kit is too much the vagrant, and perhaps too mentally disturbed, to offer much in the way of connection; Erdrich presents him, however, as an ironic counterpart to Faye. Kit is a distant relative of the Tatro clan, a firmly rooted, powerful New England family. He is convinced that his particular line of the family possesses some nebulous Native American origin; thus his goal is reverse assimilation, which he pursues with zealous determination and commitment. He tans hides, hunts local game, lives off of the land, performs tribal ceremonies, dons traditional garb, and practices his own unique brand of Native American spirituality. He struggles with an identity crisis analogous to Faye's, whose own Native identity is fraught with uncertainty. Kit marvels at Faye's revelation that her mother is "one-half Indian, that she's Ojibwe," since he thought that the women were, "like, Korean or something" (58). Erdrich presents parallel characters, one who evokes humor and the other pathos. Kit admits he is just looking for connection (5), and that is exactly what Faye is searching for as well. The sum analysis of both characters is the same: both look for an identity that is missing and struggle for a clear understanding of kinship.

When the Travers women are called to appraise the estate of the late John Jewett Tatro, a member of one of Stiles and Stokes's first families, the world of their ancestors opens up and calls them to investigate their Ojibwe heritage and their "little cat's cradle of connections" in New England and the North Dakota reservation (30). Perusing Tatro's collection of Native American artifacts, Faye looks for some stable sense of her Native American identity and contemplates her Ojibwe family history; she also discovers a startling connection between the Tatros and her maternal lineage. John Jewett Tatro's grandfather, Jewett Parker Tatro, was an Indian agent in the same Ojibwe reservation in North Dakota where her maternal grandmother was born and raised until the age of ten, "at which time she was taken east and enrolled at the Carlisle Indian

School, in Pennsylvania" (29–30). Faye notes about her grandmother that "the Carlisle Institute was also where she fell in love, or came to know her husband," and confesses that "it is hard for me to imagine that the cold little woman I remember, the anti-Grandma, I used to call her, ever fell in love or felt much in the way of human emotion" (30). Because of her one-dimensional understanding of her heritage and ancestry, she casts the grandmother as just another stock Native American character, a tribal artifact. Faye knows the story of her grandmother but seems unaware of the implications. Her grandmother's story reveals the systematic deracination of the Native American people, and Faye's lack of a stable Native American identity is a direct consequence. Because her grandmother was taken away from the reservation as a child, her descendants have little connection to their cultural heritage.

Through Faye's passing comment, Erdrich illustrates the extent to which the assimilation practices of the U.S. government threatened to erase Native American identity. Faye's lack of knowledge about Carlisle is ironic, because it exemplifies the cultural ignorance Carlisle was intended to perpetuate. Erdrich alludes to the Carlisle Indian School as a means of remembering one of the cruelest chapters of Native American history. In the late nineteenth century and into the twentieth, Native American children of all ages were removed from their homes, voluntarily or forcibly, and sent to boarding schools away from their families and tribal communities. Carlisle, the first off-reservation boarding school, was among hundreds of Indian boarding schools, both on and off the reservation, designed to assimilate Native American children. Richard Henry Pratt was the founder of Carlisle and stuck steadfastly to his motto, "Kill the Indian; Save the man." This attitude was also the driving force behind the curriculum set for the children. Tens of thousands of Native American children from all parts of the country and with various tribal affiliations were forced into an education that would better prepare them for life in the New World, their homeland, the United States. Faye recalls the story of her grandmother's own removal from the reservation: "A young teacher from Stokes, only twenty years old, had written to Tatro and was even put up at Tatro's house on the North Dakota reservation while he recruited students there. He's the one who got my grandmother to come to Carlisle. There, she learned to sew intricately, to add and subtract, to do laundry, scrub a floor clean, read, write, and recite Bible passages, Shakespeare's sonnets, Keats's odes, and the Declaration of Independence and the Bill of Rights" (30). Like all Native American children at the school, Faye's grandmother was forbidden to speak tribal languages, follow indigenous customs, practice Native American spirituality, or learn traditional skills. Instead manual labor, domestic skills, and English-language proficiency were the areas stressed, as these would prepare the children for menial positions in the world at large. All aspects of Western culture were privileged over tribal culture: language, literature, Christianity, U.S. law and government. The Indian boarding schools, serving as Western institutions of knowledge, imparted a new epistemology in line with Western cultural values. It was far cheaper to eradicate Native American culture than commit actual genocide.[7] The boarding schools, training grounds for laborers and domestic workers, worked for assimilation but not for opportunity. The U.S. government's policies on assimilation were thinly veiled attempts at deracination.[8] Faye is the trickle-down product of this forced assimilation, and yet her Native American culture survives. Erdrich makes sure of its survival by remembering the notorious Carlisle Indian Boarding School and its impact on the later generations of Ojibwe.

Another means of erasing Native American culture was the practice of some Indian agents either to trade with the tribal community for favors or to steal items outright. While serving in the capacity of Indian agent, Jewett Tatro "collected" various items from the Ojibwe, which were passed down to his heirs. Faye explains that it was not "uncommon for Indian agents to amass extensive collections of artifacts" (30). A ceremonial drum Faye finds in Tatro's cache of Ojibwe goods connects to her ancestral past. Tracing the origins of things, the lives of things, and appraising their market value is the job of the Travers women as dealers in objets d'art. Viewing artifacts only as remnants of their cultural heritage or relics from a lost lineage and culture, the Travers deal primarily in the monetary appraisal of these objects as commodities to be traded or sold. Developing a personal connection to them is taboo for their trade, yet the painted drum pulls Faye as "possessions are thought to attract the spirit back to their loved ones" (33). The drum compels her to abandon her code: "I set my hand on the drum and then I feel, pulled through me like a nerve, a clear conviction. It is visceral. Not a thought but a gut instinct" (40). She steals the drum, rationalizing that it was stolen from her ancestors. While she knows what she is doing is wrong, a crime against the heirs of Tatro, who would likely sell the collection for substantial financial gain, she reasons that the Indian Agent Tatro "walked away with everything—dolls, beadwork, cradle board. You name it" (41). The rightful heirs to these objects are the Ojibwe, so Faye thinks of the act as reclaiming her heritage rather than committing an injustice against innocents. The drum has survived its journey far from home, and Faye's recovery of it is the first step in its return. The Travers women have a stated mission to "learn its origins" and ultimately find kinship ties connecting their fates together with the Ojibwe in North Dakota. Present and future are entangled inextricably with the past, which is the fundamental theme of Erdrich's work.

In the second part of the novel, "North of Hoopdance," Erdrich develops the theme of kinship and history through the Ojibwe oral tradition of storytelling, which is a key feature of this part of the novel. Healing and remembering are the themes of the story and also the dual purpose of the ceremonial drum. Bernard Shaawano is the storyteller, driven, for historical and personal reasons, to relay the story to Faye and Elsie, who have traveled to the reservation. It is a lesson in Shaawano and Pillager clan history as well as a personal family history for the Travers women, whose connection to the community is investigated by Geraldine Coutts, recorder of the tribal history of the reservation: "they are connected to an old branch of the Pillagers through a girl who escaped the sicknesses here by going to that eastern school, Carlisle, where they took so many of us at one time" (102). The interconnected history of the Ojibwe families reveals the Travers women's connection to the drum, to Bernard, and to the reservation.

The inspiration for the drum, or the need for its creation, arises from the story in the second chapter of part 2, "The Shawl."[9] Bernard is the storyteller because he received a firsthand account of the tale from his father, Old Shaawano. In sum the story takes place in the early days of settlement, in the mid-1800s, when various Ojibwe communities still possessed tribal land and their traditional ways of life. The main impact of colonialism depicted in this short story is the suffering of Bernard's grandfather, also named Shaawano, who suffers from tuberculosis, one of the many devastating consequences of contact with Euro-American settlers. The central concern of the story is not colonialism, however, but the betrayal committed by Shaawano's wife, Anaquot, the mother of his two children, a nine-year-old daughter and a five-year-old boy who eventually becomes Bernard's father and keeper of the drum. Anaquot, Bernard's grandmother, becomes pregnant as a result of a sexual relationship with Simon Jack Pillager, a trader from a neighboring Ojibwe community, and ultimately gives birth to their daughter. Anaquot cannot bear to be without her lover, so she decides to abandon her family and pursue a future with Simon Jack. One night she absconds with her eldest child, her daughter with Shaawano, and the baby to join Simon Jack and his Pillager clan. During her escape in the dead of winter, hungry wolves chase the horse-drawn cart, driven by a kinsman of Ziigwan'aage, Simon Jack's wife. In a desperate moment, as the wolves close in on the cart, the elder daughter jumps off the back as a sacrifice to save her family, particularly the baby sister she so loves. The wolves pick her bones clean, and Shaawano later finds the fragile bones of his beloved daughter, collects them, and eventually makes a ceremonial drum, in which he places those bones, as a means of healing and remembering her sacrifice. The drum not only becomes a means of healing Shaawano's emotional trauma but also gains attention throughout the community as an instrument for healing all manner of illness; thus the young girl's sacrifice ultimately brings the Ojibwe community together.

The story of the painted drum, then, is finally one of survival, even though it deals with death: of a family, of a child, of a traditional way of life. This positive interpretation holds that the story champions the indelible interconnectedness among the Ojibwe, the complex system of kinship, and the hard-won survival of the people and their culture in the face of dispossession and deracination. Faye learns from Bernard's account that his family line tangles with her own. Her grandmother is the daughter of Simon Jack, which makes Elsie Simon Jack's granddaughter. Bernard's grandmother is Anaquot, Simon Jack's lover and mother of his child. The most interesting revelation for readers of Erdrich's Love Medicine series, however, is the fact that the love child of Anaquot and Simon Jack is Fleur Pillager, a central character in Erdrich's oeuvre. Erdrich adds another line to the intricate genealogy of her fictional reservation. Upon entering Erdrich's fictional world, readers must make constant "revisions to family history" (29) and realize that "there is no telling when one event will stop bumping into the next" (65). In a characteristically interwoven family tree, Faye is actually deeply connected to the characters in the Love Medicine series. She is the half grandniece of Fleur, who is also Elsie's half aunt. Fleur's own father was Elsie's grandfather. Through generations of dispossession and deracination, Fleur's Pillager line persists. The little boy ultimately becomes Bernard's father, Old Shaawano, who attempts to drink away the memory of the haunting story of his family's breakdown and trades away the painted drum to Jewett Tatro for alcohol, another consequence of settlement. Old Shaawano tells the story again and again to anyone who will hear it in order to find peace. While the story of the drum and of Anaquot does not directly concern the impact of colonialism, it stands as a reminder of Ojibwe survival in connections of kinship that remain intact through oppression and erasure, dispossession and deracination. Tragedy is averted with Faye's discovery and reclamation of a vital part of her family history, the painted drum, and consequently her identity.

Healing is the prevailing theme of the third and fourth parts of the novel, in which Erdrich depicts the enduring impact of the painted drum on two geographically distant yet culturally and spiritually connected communities. Departing from the Faye Travers story, the third section of the novel reveals the authentic healing power of the drum in the Ojibwe community. Now that the drum has found its way back to the reservation, Bernard's family inheritance is recovered, and the drum reclaims its original purpose and rightful place in the community. Analogous to the drum's survival and return to its roots, the

Ojibwe who believe in the old ways and the traditional means of healing also persevere. Bernard communicates the story of the drum's return in a letter to Faye, back in New Hampshire, in the fourth and final part of novel. Though Faye and Elsie return to the East Coast, they share a renewed interest in their Ojibwe roots and even speculate about returning to the reservation permanently someday. The reservation in North Dakota will always offer community and an authentic sense of home for these two displaced tribal members. In a characteristic display of trickster humor, Erdrich reveals, once Faye is back in New Hampshire, that her fellow soul searcher in the neighborhood, Kit Tatro, has reconnected with his roots as well. While he is driving on the highway, a Jeep Cherokee almost runs him off the road, but a Winnebago prevents the accident. Predictably Kit takes this as a sign of his Winnebago, or "Ho-Chunk," origins, which Kit informs Faye is the preferred designation of his recently adopted Native American tribal community (266). Erdrich believes it is within the power of every individual to construct a narrative that reflects an authentically felt identity. The ability to take control, finally, of one's own story is ultimately a healing thing.

CHAPTER 3

Tracks, Four Souls, and *The Last Report on the Miracles at Little No Horse*

Louise Erdrich's writing is politically charged; moreover, through the use of experimentation, she reflects the history and politics of the Ojibwe, arguably more effectively than she could in a more conventionally realistic novel. Whereas the multiple narrators of *Love Medicine* effectively present a picture of life on the reservation spanning the twentieth century, *Tracks* (1988) most explicitly exposes the split in Ojibwe identity, a result of early historical tensions between the colonized and the colonizers, through her dual, at times dueling, narrators. *Tracks* successfully incorporates narrative experimentation to achieve political ends. Erdrich's use of multiple narrators does not undermine her understanding or presentation of the Ojibwe people; rather it highlights the subjectivity of the Ojibwe and the complexity of their existence. Deborah Stead explains how Erdrich arrived at the narrative technique she uses in the novel: "The tale was unlocked only when she finally found the right way to tell it. 'Michael [Dorris] started talking about the Athapaskin Indians who live around Tyonek, Alaska, where he once hunted. In their language, there is no word for 'I'—only 'we.'"[1] Erdrich opted for multiple narrators in *Tracks* to dramatize the fact that the autonomous individual in Ojibwe life, as in the Athapaskin community, is nonexistent.

There is no dominant truth one can communicate that serves as a sweeping summation of Ojibwe existence; there is no master narrative. To reduce the life of a people to one voice, one narrator, in spite of the chorus of voices sounding on and off the reservation would be misleading. Erdrich's experimental choice to use two narrators is the most effective way to communicate the diversity of Ojibwe life, particularly in crisis and in flux. Thus the ostensible big truth of

Native American identity and history that Erdrich uncovers in *Tracks* is that there is no such big truth or totalizing narrative. The desire by the dominant culture to find the grand narrative of Native American life can even be seen in certain reviews of the novel. *Tracks* received positive reviews,[2] but some reviewers tended to miss the novel's little, local truths offered in search of larger themes. Dan Cryer concluded a generally praising review with a qualification concerning Erdrich's characters: "Someday, I think, Louise Erdrich will figure out a way to make each character's voice more distinctive. . . . Each narrator, however, is too much the poet, too eager to turn a phrase to be wholly individualized." Cryer called this lack of individualized characters the novel's biggest flaw and asserted that it is "a persistent one in Erdrich's work."[3] What Cryer considered a flaw, however, is in fact precisely what Erdrich intended: highly stylized depictions of the Ojibwe people.

Identity is fluid; history is negotiable. These are the two persistent themes in *Tracks* embodied by its two narrators, Nanapush and Pauline. Each character offers a unique history of life in and around their Ojibwe reservation bordering Argus, North Dakota, in the years 1912–24. During this time there was great upheaval in the tribe as disease, famine, U.S. government land allotment acts, and Christianity simultaneously overwhelmed the community. Nanapush, a community elder and namesake of the trickster figure Nanabozho in Ojibwe myth, tells his story to stave off the complete annihilation of his native culture in the face of all this adversity. Erdrich positions him in the novel as a counterpoint to the grand narratives of Western history that attempt to define and construct Native American identity and history. Nanapush's mission is to provide the reader and his adopted granddaughter, Lulu, to whom he is telling the story, with petite narratives, deeply felt personal truths, in order to preserve his Ojibwe culture. Pauline, a mixed-blood, strives to assimilate with the dominant culture and validate the grand narratives it promotes. Nanapush says it best while describing those who generate the constant onslaught of rumors and speculations surrounding Fleur Pillager, Lulu's mother and the primary focus in both his and Pauline's narratives: "It comes up different every time, and has no ending, no beginning. They get the middle wrong too. They only know they don't know anything."[4] In this passage Nanapush is referring particularly to Pauline, who has willingly abandoned her Ojibwe roots in hopes of fully assimilating into the Western, specifically Catholic, community. Nanapush understands that it is the Western need for linearity and finality that motivates Pauline's ideas, and her narrative, about Fleur. But Nanapush will not allow Pauline's simple summation of events to obscure his narrative, for it is only through the interplay of small stories that an appropriate depiction of Ojibwe life can be created.

Native American history, as well as identity, is perpetuated through its discourse, its stories. These stories consist of oral histories, local myths, and family fictions. In order to offer a "realistic" version of Ojibwe existence, Erdrich effectively uses dual narrators in alternating chapters that act as a buffer for one another. By not privileging one narrator over the other—neither narrator can claim absolute authenticity—Erdrich creates a novel that reflects the diverse and often diametrically opposed realities of Ojibwe life. By using two distinct and conflicting narrators, Nanapush and Pauline, Erdrich is able to create a tension similar to that surrounding the crisis of history and identity, a real struggle for survival that the Ojibwe were feeling in the early part of the twentieth century.

Erdrich's use of two narrators highlights the fact that the Ojibwe were a divided people during the time of *Tracks*. Steven Scott agrees that at this specific time in their history, the Ojibwe were "indeed 'a people of two worlds,' striving to keep a dying culture alive, and striving at the same time to cope with a surging white culture determined to either change them or submerge them."[5] Scott speculates that there are "at least two novels at work here," which is at once experimental and conventionally Native American in its narrative quality.[6] These two novels are narrated alternatingly by representatives of each world, traditional and pervasively white.

Nanapush, a full-blooded Ojibwe, acts as storyteller and spokesperson for the Ojibwe whose community is jeopardized by the infusion of white culture in the form of legal documents, paper money, and government—in sum, capitalism. During the course of the novel, he is telling Lulu, his adopted granddaughter, the story of her full-blooded Ojibwe mother, Fleur Pillager, and of the Ojibwe's struggle to keep their community and land intact in the face of unrelenting disease and famine, questionable land allotments, exorbitant taxes, and unfair fees: "Granddaughter, you are the child of the invisible" (1). Nanapush is referring to the fact that the Pillagers succumbed to the "spotted disease," smallpox, which devastated their clan in the winter of 1912. Fleur, Lulu's mother, was the only Pillager to survive and carry on the clan's traditions. Now Nanapush, though he has his doubts, hopes that Lulu will do the same. Lulu has been away for most of the action of Nanapush's story at a government school, an Indian boarding school where most of her education has come by way of white Christian educators. By infusing her with the power and energy of her native people through their stories, Nanapush wishes to empower Lulu in the face of the competing narratives she has been exposed to that serve to diminish or taint the history of the Ojibwe. However he must struggle to keep Lulu's attention. At several times during the course of his narrative, he stops to admonish her for not possessing her mother's reverence and interest in his stories: "Even when I bored her, she made a good effort at pretending some interest. She never tapped her fingers on her uncovered knees, shuffled and twisted and made faces out the window like you" (178). Lulu does not have the reverence or respect that Fleur had for her elders. But Nanapush forges ahead with the story, for he believes that only through storytelling can he keep his whole community from falling into obscurity or invisibility.

In the long-held Ojibwe tradition of oral storytelling, an effective method of constructing history and preserving identity, Nanapush is saving the last remnants of his tribe through his stories: "They're all attached, and once I start there is no end to telling because they're hooked from one side to the other, mouth to tail. During the year of sickness, when I was the last one left, I saved myself by starting a story" (46). So Nanapush, like Fleur, is the last in a long line of full-blooded clans. In a turn reminiscent of the *Arabian Nights,* he realizes that only through the telling of their story will his people and culture persist. In a poignant moment, Nanapush reflects on the significance of ostensibly being the end of the line: "I guided the last buffalo hunt. I saw the last bear shot. I trapped the last beaver with a pelt of more than two years' growth. I spoke aloud the words of the government treaty, and refused to sign the settlement papers that would take away our woods and lake. I axed the last birch that was older than I, and I saved the last Pillager" (2). Nanapush is painfully aware of his position as the last witness of many of the rituals and traditions of the Ojibwe. Thus he takes on the great responsibility of preserving the culture of his people with unmitigated vigor.

In the same passage, he confesses to Lulu: "My girl, I saw the passing of times you will never know" (2). Even though he takes his time to relay meticulously the events of the past few years to Lulu, Nanapush resigns himself to the undeniable fact that the old way of life is gone forever for future generations of Ojibwe; only a small piece of this history will survive in Lulu's memory if she chooses to retain it. He also realizes his inability to communicate a complete understanding of the import of the events of the past to this outsider, much as Erdrich must when taking on the project of writing a novel such as *Tracks.* The whole story can never be told, only parts. And even if it could be told, it would never be fully understood by those who did not experience it. This arguably postmodern awareness of the pitfalls of literary representation, the inefficacy of transmitting big truths, is at the heart of Nanapush's frustration. However history, particularly in the Native American sense, is a deeply personal but also communal narrative of events. Obviously, then, if storytelling is the means by which history is transmitted, it is highly debatable and open to interpretation. Those who offer up their private oral histories often understand the tenuous nature of such narratives but are reassured that all other stories are then subject to the same scrutiny. It is the duty of the informed listener or reader to decide what pieces or which story to accept or reject. Likewise the teller of a story also has a duty to include other versions.

Erdrich shares an alternate version of the events in Argus through a second narrator, Pauline Puyat, a mixed-blood, part Ojibwe and part Canadian, member of the community. Pauline struggles throughout the novel to come to terms with the identification she feels with the full-blooded natives she shares a history with and the Catholic nuns she has tried to assimilate with as a prodigal daughter of sorts. This violent yoking of incompatible cultures results in an increasing emotional and psychological instability. She ultimately turns to old Ojibwe magic and extreme Christian zeal to negotiate her way through this deeply divided community. Pauline, unlike Nanapush, is not telling a story to a listener who is present. One can surmise that she is writing her story rather than speaking it aloud. This is one of the chief differences between Pauline's and Nanapush's narratives. Pauline does not embrace or enlist her Ojibwe storytelling capacities but eschews them for the Western, linear, documentary style of conveying history. Unaware of her growing insanity, she never hesitates or questions the reliability of her account of the events because she is giving her own deeply personal interpretation of the past. Though the reader may sense her unreliability and perhaps the alarming rate at which she is spiraling out of control, Pauline's version is valid because it is *hers*—her internalized version of the truth, her subjective, deeply personal narrative. She is documenting the events as only she can process them. The account is largely uncontested, for Erdrich does not editorialize or silence Pauline's narrative but gives her roughly an equal number of pages as Nanapush to relay and complete her story. Erdrich lets her have her say, for it is only through alternative and even conflicting narratives that readers can arrive at a richer, more complex picture of the history of the Ojibwe.

Pauline begins her narrative with an account of her life before the brutal winter of 1912, which begins Nanapush's narrative: "We were mixed-bloods, skinners in the clan for which the name was lost. In the spring before the winter that took so many Ojibwe, I bothered my father into sending me south, to the white town. I had decided to learn the lace-making trade from nuns" (14). Right away Pauline's dislocation and isolation from the community is evident. Where Nanapush is elegiac and reverent in tone describing the terrific loss suffered by his people that winter, Pauline's interest lies outside the community with the Catholic nuns, and her narrative reflects her emotional and physical distance from the Ojibwe. Instead of putting emphasis on the *we* of the Ojibwe, her focus is on *I*, an individual apart from her people. Pauline's distancing from her Ojibwe heritage is a recurrent phenomenon for Erdrich's divided and/or intensely assimilated characters. Furthermore this passage illustrates Pauline's mixed-blood ancestry, which is at the heart of her fragmentation and alienation from both the Ojibwe and the European worlds. Through the character of Pauline, Erdrich symbolizes the significant spiritual and cultural rift manifest in so many of the Ojibwe as a result of colonization and assimilation practices.

Before Pauline travels south, her father warns her that she will "fade out there" because she is lighter than her sisters. He recognizes her unsteady connection with the Ojibwe and ventures to prophesize that she "won't be an Indian" once she returns (14). Pauline agrees: "I wanted to be like my grandfather, pure Canadian. That was because even as a child I saw that to hang back was to perish" (14). This privileging of the self—this self-centeredness—is in direct opposition to the traditional Ojibwe idea of community and communal living. Nanapush chooses to hang back in order to save his Ojibwe heritage, but Pauline wants to flee and save herself. Again this passage reflects Pauline's transition to a more Western, capitalist, and ultimately solipsistic way of being. By the end of her narrative, she seems only mildly cognizant of the external world of the Ojibwe; she focuses her awareness on her own existence, her "whiteness," and her personal relationship with God, which so skews her perception of reality that she can no longer conceive of any other way of being than her own. The plight of the Ojibwe is of no pressing concern to her. She only senses that they will lose their land due to their stubborn lack of assimilation. Furthermore where Nanapush is concerned with the future generations of the community, Pauline has written them off, for they "return from the government schools blinded and deafened" (205). Echoing her own blindness and deafness, the younger members of the tribe, including Lulu, have from Pauline's perspective become irreversibly acculturated. As the reverent zealot, she rejoices for them, because only through an acceptance of the white world and a deep communion with their Catholic God can they be saved. Thus the division between Pauline and Nanapush is further brought to the fore in terms of their views on salvation. Nanapush believes that only through narrating the history of the Ojibwe to Lulu can he preserve his culture; Pauline utilizes her narrative to proselytize, to extol the virtues of Christian living for the disenfranchised mixed-bloods and the incorrigible full Ojibwe, thereby ensuring salvation.

Though Pauline seems to accept fully her new Catholic identity, ironically she continues to struggle with, and put stock in, the myths and legends—the stories—of the Ojibwe. Her preoccupation with Fleur for the greater part of her narrative discloses her insecurity with her new community of nuns and her jealousy of Fleur's full-blood status with its attendant sexuality, animalism, and mystery. Fleur is figured as an archetypal, mythic Native American in Pauline's narrative, much like the depictions of Native Americans in Western literature. The inscrutability and confusion surrounding Fleur illustrates Pauline's disconnection from her roots—Fleur is something "other" rather than a member of Pauline's own Ojibwe community. Furthermore Fleur's connection to nature, particularly to her plot of land and to natural life in the form of raw sexuality, are a constant source of envy for Pauline. At many points in her narrative, she reports on the mystifying life and personage of Fleur, rife with violence, peculiar sexuality, and magical trickster-like abilities: Fleur gambles with male coworkers in an Argus butcher shop and is gang-raped by them when they lose a substantial amount of money to her (26); she almost destroys the town by "causing" a tornado (28); she allegedly is the land bride of a mythical water creature called Misshepeshu and births his child (31); she is a shapeshifter who takes the form of an animal at night to hunt for food (12). Much of Pauline's testimony reflects a disconnection with Fleur and her way of life and, in no small measure, jealousy and grudging admiration. Fleur is a strong, independent full-blooded Ojibwe; Pauline is a weak, nervous, and confused mixed-blood. Fleur carries the pride that comes with her name—Pillager. Pauline cares little about her heritage and relinquishes her name for the name the Mother Superior at her convent has picked for her—Leopolda (205). Fleur's legacy lives on in the story of her life and through her daughter, Lulu. Pauline's only legacy is administering last rites to the dead of Argus: "I handled the dead until the cold feel of their skin was a comfort, until I no longer bothered to bathe once I left the cabin but touched others with the same hands, passed death on" (69). In sum Fleur is full of vitality, while Pauline is metaphorically, spiritually, emotionally, and culturally dead.

Yet the sympathetic reader feels some sense of Pauline's vitality in her strong commitment to her version of the story. Though she cannot conceive of another reality, she remains focused on telling her story because she believes in an unnamed and mystical connection with Fleur. Pauline and Fleur, at least to Pauline, are strange counterparts. Fleur is the last vestige of the Pillager clan, and Pauline is the last in her line. Furthermore Pauline is obsessed with telling Fleur's story even though it ultimately takes a subordinate position to her own life story and her relationship with God: "I was no longer jealous or afraid of her, but . . . became her moving shadow that the men never noticed, the shadow that could have saved her" (22). Like Nanapush, with his desire to save his culture, Pauline also has a wish to save Fleur, and this in part drives her narrative. Unfortunately this desire stems from an almost colonialist need to conquer the unknown or stamp out the unknowable rather than a sincere concern for the welfare of others or the preservation of a people and their culture. She pursues, meddles with, and judges Fleur with all of the rigor and stamina of a religious zealot or an imperialist.

Pauline's religious zeal reveals a disturbing yet curious connection to the ways in which Native American life was infiltrated by the Western Christian world. She is continually being "visited" by God; he seems to have a special mission for her. The scenes of communion between God and Pauline illustrate her increasing madness. God always picks quite mundane, though humorous, places to make an appearance to her. One night she sees him sitting on the kitchen stove: "He said that I was not whom I had supposed. I was an orphan and my parents had died in grace, and also, despite my deceptive features, I was not one speck of Indian but wholly white" (137). However these passages serve a twofold purpose. Not only do they illustrate Pauline's delusions and paranoia (God is everywhere and sees everything she does) and desire to be pious, but they also demonstrate her wish to be, as Erdrich cleverly plays with homonyms, "wholly white." Aside from the absurdity of this passage, the import of God delivering a message of white supremacy to Pauline should not be underestimated.

Of course Pauline's greatest dream is to be white, and by worshipping a white God, she distances herself from her Ojibwe roots and embraces a decidedly Western way of being. By attaching whiteness to piety or conflating the idea of whiteness with holiness, she symbolizes the cultural dislocation of many Ojibwe and the subversive way in which the Western world employed religion for imperialist ends. In fact by the end of her narrative, Pauline completely disconnects from the Ojibwe community and focuses on saving the evil, misguided "Indians," no longer using the proper names of the tribes and referring to them with the third-person *them* rather than the self-inclusive *us* (138). Through Pauline, Erdrich offers a character who serves as a testament to those Ojibwe who suffered untold humiliation, confusion, and psychological, emotional, and spiritual fragmentation trying to balance on a cultural hinge between two diametrically opposed worlds. The poignant struggle to come to terms with one's "nativeness" in light of encroaching Western Christian culture and to survive in this new culture is effectively depicted in Pauline's narrative. Her identity crisis, though framed in terms of religious fanaticism and psychological instability, represents a very real part of Ojibwe existence during the time period of the novel. However the true impact of this kind of emotional struggle can only be felt when considered in the context of the numerous and varied political and economic hardships of the Ojibwe.

While Pauline's narrative centers on the identity crisis felt by many Ojibwe, Nanapush's narrative exposes the toll this fragmentation of the tribe and general cultural confusion took on the economic situation of the Ojibwe. Where the cultural values of his people dictated that a man's word was the only contract needed or that a tacit understanding of tradition would "legally" suffice,

Nanapush discovers that in the white world, bureaucracy and red tape are the order of the day, and deception and self-interest are the key motivations behind any deal. Unlike Pauline, who freely and actively seeks acceptance in this new world, Nanapush holds out for as long as he can. He remains loyal to his people and culture in the face of steady government pressure to assimilate, sign shady treaties, and give up the land.

Nanapush is no pushover. He questions the motives of the government agents, since he knows the consequences of blindly entering into agreements with them. Even the seemingly simple and harmless act of signing his name to a contract that he approves of causes him alarm: "Nanapush is a name that loses power every time it is written and stored in a government file. That is why I only gave it out once in all those years" (32). He realizes that giving one's name to the government never ends in a good way. A name loses its meaning each time it is written because the name ultimately replaces the identity of the person it describes. Names serve to pigeonhole and never capture the true essence of an individual if overused or stored away in a government file. Finally the individual exists in name only and not as a living, breathing person. In order to avoid this erasure of identity, the wily Nanapush instead offers "No Name" as his moniker to any government agents or church representatives (32). Unfortunately his steps to ensure the preservation of his people and culture are insufficient to keep the land intact. Because of the sustained strain of poverty and disease, his people need fast money to purchase food and medicine. Commerce takes the shape of cold capitalism, replacing the communal bartering system of the Ojibwe. Land becomes the people's only commodity. Speaking of cash agreements between the government agents and his tribesmen for land, Nanapush realizes the colossal mistake his tribesmen are making: "I know this. Land is the only thing that lasts life to life. Money burns like tinder, flows off like water. And as for government promises, the wind is steadier" (33). He draws the correct conclusion. The cash agreements and contracts bring further debt and taxes to the Ojibwe and leave them in greater need. The land is lost, never to be recovered.

The loss of land and culture devastate many in the Ojibwe community. Any autonomy or liberty they once possessed disappeared along with the land and the old way of doing things. The reservation is diminished. Butchered forests, lumber companies, internal strife, and illegal taxes replace "lost times when game was plenty, companions sharp with humor, times when it would have taken four days to walk the length of this reservation" (191). The destruction of the community leads to an attitude of capitalist self-interest. The capitalist system, with its papers and documents and taxes, has replaced the tribal way of living. Nanapush immediately realizes the course his tribesmen are charting for themselves as soon as the government agents and the lumber companies appear: "That's when I began to see what we were becoming, and the years have borne me out: a tribe of file cabinets and triplicates, a tribe of single-space documents, directives, policy. A tribe of pressed trees. A tribe of chicken-scratch that can be scattered by a wind, diminished to ashes by one struck match" (225). Sadly Nanapush can do nothing about the economic adversity his people must face. However he can continue to create or reconstruct the identity of his people for the younger generation through his stories. Hoping that the Ojibwe children are not "so full of what they see in the mirror" (170), the tribal elders may be able to reach the minds and hearts of the young Ojibwe and instill in them a sense of pride and an urgency to preserve their rich culture.

Erdrich, also through storytelling, attempts to preserve her people's cultural heritage. She offers not a totalizing narrative of Ojibwe experience and history but two widely varying and conflicting "little" narratives that combine to create a full picture of reservation life. Her creation of these competing narratives lends her credibility absent in several of the superficial and one-dimensional portraits of Native Americans. The refusal to package a nice and neat narrative with easily interpretable themes, characters, and storylines signals a political move. Erdrich revises the notion of Native American identity, one created by the dominant culture, and replaces it with a more real characterization of the Ojibwe. She reconstructs Native American identity so that the term may capture a multiplicity of subjectivities and histories rather than be relegated to one or two big truths that signify nothing in lived Ojibwe existence. Finally Erdrich does this through experimental narrative strategies rather than traditional realistic techniques, for those strategies afford her the specific tools and parameters to best achieve her political goals.

Four Souls

Set in the twin cities of Minneapolis–Saint Paul, *Four Souls* (2004) continues the story of Fleur where *Tracks* ends. Fleur leaves the reservation in North Dakota and heads to Saint Paul to exact revenge on the lumber baron John James Mauser, who stole her land and razed the trees for lumber. As in *Tracks,* Erdrich primarily uses dual narrators. In this novel Nanapush and the European American Polly Elizabeth Gheen weave the story from remnants that they collect personally or from conversations with others who encountered Fleur during the time she was away from the reservation, creating a full picture culled from various little narratives. The reader is presented with a characteristic Erdrich narrative that may or may not tell the whole story but gives a sense of events, of this slice of Fleur's history, from various vantage points. Erdrich investigates the themes of revenge and justice, loss and recovery, and identity and self-awareness, all in the context of Fleur's mission to avenge the loss of her ancestral land. Nanapush takes up the story from the reservation, presenting the Ojibwe perspective, which he patches together with the help of his wife, Margaret (Rushes Bear), who narrates small portions of the novel; Father Damien; and Fleur herself, years after the events. In his inimitable wily tone, Nanapush admits that he had to "piece together" the story: "Sometimes an old man doesn't know how he knows things. He can't remember where knowledge came from. Sometimes it is clear. . . . My long talks with Father Damien resulted in a history of the great house that Fleur grinned up at that day. . . . During those long conversations, Father Damien and I exchanged rumors, word, and speculation about Fleur's life. . . . We guessed that she followed her trees and, from that, we grew convinced that she was determined to cut down the man who took them. She had lived among those oak and pine trees when their roots grew deep beneath her and their leaves thick above. Now he lived among them, too, only he lived among them cut and dead."[7] Nanapush and Father Damien guess correctly. Fleur has gone off to bring down the house of Mauser.

The theme of dispossession, a consequence of settlement, is central, with Fleur attempting against all odds to avenge the dispossession of her land and win it back. Erdrich explicitly reveals the consequences of the colonization of Ojibwe territory: settlement was about not only loss of the land but also of the loss of the *spirit* of the land and the ancestral history diminished by its taking. The loss of the clan's homestead is a psychic and physical trauma for Fleur, as that land represents her way of life, her means of living, and her complete communion with the landscape. Fleur retains the mythic and mysterious countenance established in *Tracks,* but a weakness is revealed in this novel. The single-minded focus on revenge, the power of that desire, isolates Fleur from her Ojibwe family, community, and culture. Her keen attention to her goal admits no distractions; not even the welfare of her daughter Lulu concerns her. Fleur abandons her to a government boarding school, the trauma of which is described in *Love Medicine,* and leaves Lulu to the care of Nanapush and Margaret once the girl's education is completed. The passion that compels her to seek revenge springs from the same source as the self-righteousness—her unwavering pride. There is no question that Fleur's land was stolen from her through shady land deals and taxes imposed by the government, but the sting is all the more bitter because she is a victim of the scam. Fleur is no wilting flower—never a victim. From the circumstances of her birth straight through to the time of her death, the events of which are discussed in various novels, Fleur is arguably Erdrich's greatest Ojibwe survivor, rivaled only by Nanapush, and possesses unshakeable confidence in her independence and self-sufficiency.

In his narrative Nanapush empathizes with Fleur, as he has seen the consequences of colonization and settlement firsthand. He describes the systematic destruction of Ojibwe land in the interest of harvesting the abundant natural resources: vegetable, mineral (rock and metal), and animal. An onslaught of land developers and real estate entrepreneurs stripped Ojibwe land of brownstone, basswood, oak, pine, copper, soapstone, slate, pyrite, iron, water, and wildlife (5–7). The destination for these materials was Gakaabikaang, the Ojibwe word for Minneapolis, in order to develop the infrastructure of the city and its great buildings, including mansions and factories.[8] While raising their cities, the settlers leveled Ojibwe territory. Here Erdrich reveals the extent to which settlers robbed the Ojibwe; it was not just the land they stole, but everything the land contained in its depths. The deep wound carved into the land would never fully heal for the Ojibwe. Though treaties were made, reservations established, and allotments assigned, the original homestead of the Ojibwe was irrevocably lost, and with it a centuries old way of life. This fracturing of the land required a new way of thinking about survival and existence and also a new way of knowing the world at large and one's place in it. Erdrich's body of fiction is instrumental in bringing this cataclysmic ontological and epistemological shift to light for her readers, symbolized in such events as the building of Mauser's great mansion.

Erdrich's description of Mauser's mansion reveals the results of dispossession and is the novel's central symbol of that dispossession. In the course of Nanapush's narration, the house is described as the product of blood, sweat, and tears:

> They had this house of chimneys whose bricks contained the blood of pigs and calves so that a greasy sadness drifted in the festive rooms. . . . This house of tears of lace constructed of a million tiny knots of useless knowledge . . . this house of windows hung with the desperations of dark virgins . . . this house of stacked sandstone colored the richest clay-red and lavender hue. Once this stone had formed the live heart of sacred islands . . . this house of shame . . . this house of railroad and then lumber money and the sucking grind of eastern mills . . . this house of lead plumbing that eroded minds . . . this house of beeswaxed mantels and carved paneling . . . of wood, fine-grained, very old-grown, quartersawn oak that still in its season and from many years after would exude beads of thin sap—as though recalling growth and life on the land belonging to Fleur Pillager and the shores of Matchimanito, beyond. (8–9)

Erdrich highlights the insensitive and impersonal nature of the construction of the mansion, which pays no respect or debt to the sacred essence of the land

and its resources. The callousness with which every part of the house is built, with which the various parts of the land are utilized, adds an additional layer of insult to the Ojibwe. The architectural finery, the furniture, and the structure itself, down to the foundation, are built from the spoils of Fleur's land. Surely Erdrich is creating an impression of the lengths to which the colonizers relied on the resources of the Ojibwe, and Native Americans in general, for their livelihoods. Furthermore there is no talent other than capitalistic market skills for hostile takeovers and the ability to press the advantage of loopholes in federal policies that accounts for this. The law is on the side of the settlers because of its fluidity, the liberties taken by clever entrepreneurs, and the failure of the government to protect the land rights of Native Americans. These land-grabbing practices are carried out with impunity. The resulting frenzy is akin to a modern real estate bubble that, unfortunately for the Ojibwe, never experiences the inevitable burst. Mauser strips the land of natural resources, then "flips" it for profit, a time-honored capitalist practice. He develops no connection to the land other than recognizing its monetary value and resources, viewing it only as property. Whereas the Ojibwe worship the land, view it as sacred, and honor their deep communion with it, Mauser looks upon the land as a possession to be used and discarded. To that extent the great house is more profoundly a part of Fleur, of her cultural makeup, than of Mauser, even before she takes her first step inside.

Fleur's arrival and time in the Mauser household is recounted by the other main narrator of the novel, Polly Elizabeth Gheen, Mauser's sister-in-law, who takes up the narration in the twin cities of Minneapolis and Saint Paul. Her narration provides the non-Native or colonial perspective, as is seen clearly through her description of the house: "On the most exclusive ridge of the city, our pure white house was set, pristine as a cake in the window of a bakery shop. High on sloped and snowy grounds, it was unshadowed yet by trees. The roof, gables, porch, all chiseled and bored in fantastic shapes . . . the white cast-iron benches . . . the white deer at the gate . . . pawed delicately at its pedestal" (11). Polly Elizabeth conflates the ideas of purity and "whiteness" in her vision of the house, contrary to the dark description of it offered by Nanapush. That it is "unshadowed" by trees or foliage is an irony, since the razing of the trees of the landscape to build the house is noted as a positive attribute. The statue of a deer, also white, serves as a rough substitute for the majesty of the wildlife that once populated the land. All of Polly Elizabeth's observations illustrate her disconnection from and objectification of her surroundings and a marked absence of vitality—all the images are of inanimate forms and shapes. Even her description of Fleur's arrival objectifies and detracts: "I see the negative of her as she stooped to her dark bundle, the image of a question mark set on a page, alone. . . . the deep black figure draped in shawls was more an absence" (12). Her immediate identification of "negative" with "dark," qualities she ascribes to Native Americans generally, stands in direct contrast to the whiteness that permeates Polly Elizabeth's life. She confesses that she was caught up in the "appearance of her" (12) rather than calculating the risk she might pose to the Mauser household. Paying little heed to Fleur, an "absence" beneath her notice, Polly Elizabeth explains: "Indians are unintelligible, to the civilized mind I mean, as far removed in habit of thought and behavior as wild wolves from bred hounds" (14). This stereotypical, one-dimensional perspective, comparing Native Americans to animals in intellect and action, is yet another stark example of the racist attitudes pervasive in the Euro-American community. Fleur seemingly has "no family connections," which pleases Polly Elizabeth, as this permits any kind of treatment by her employers, ensures Fleur's dependence on a steady income, and eases any threat of retribution from family members seeking to advocate on her behalf. Aloneness is preferable; of course Polly Elizabeth has underestimated the power of this singular woman.

Contrary to Ojibwe values, Fleur does act as an individual, without connections, until the last chapters of the novel. Her sole desire is retribution, to ruin Mauser, which is ultimately the literal and figurative result of her time in the Twin Cities. The price of revenge, however, is that she loses sight of herself and her culture for a number of years. Erdrich does not offer one-dimensional characters, and Fleur is undoubtedly one of her most complex, multilayered creations. No character is absolutely a victim, and no avenging angel is without fault in Erdrich's fiction. While Fleur does infiltrate Mauser's household, manages to seduce him with her powers of healing and her untamed, natural passion, and succeeds in deposing Placide Gheen, his frail and sexually dysfunctional wife, she does not exact her bloody revenge and slit his throat in the night. Instead she rises to an unforeseen level of power as the new Mrs. John James Mauser. Fleur rationalizes entering into this union with Mauser because when she first arrived at the house, his life was spiraling downhill: "Mauser already suffered, she felt cheated of her revenge. She wanted the man healthy so that she could destroy him fresh" (24). For someone plotting the perfect act of revenge, this makes sense; supporting Mauser was "the only honorable way a Pillager could take satisfaction in vengeance" (73). Nonetheless Fleur's newly acquired social status in Mauser's community brings her such pleasure that onlookers wonder if she has forgotten her initial purpose. She is "snagged," "dazzled," and "temporarily fascinated" by the "high life" and the "rich swirl of chimookomanag [white man's] doings and foods" particularly the "smoked white sturgeon at the party given in her honor at their wedding" (74). She immerses herself in the mainstream culture of Mauser circle, with some success. Closely observing the rituals of this new community, Fleur hosts parties, attends social events, dresses in the finest Western fashions, and relishes the gourmet cuisine. Predictably she is not accepted as one of their own but is considered something other, a foreigner, an Indian: "Certainly, she had to know that people called her squaw behind her back," reasons Polly Elizabeth. Not only is this a sign of the deep-seated racism leveled at the Ojibwe, but it also serves as an indictment to proponents of assimilation, who posit that Native Americans will be welcomed into Western culture and society seamlessly.

Nanapush even speculates that perhaps Fleur's arrogance has blinded her to the true nature of the man with whom she is now cohabitating, as he knows well Mauser's history with the Ojibwe: "he had married young Ojibwe girls straight out of boarding school, applied for their permits to log off the allotment lands they had inherited. Once their trees were gone he had abandoned his young wives, one after the next. . . . He took the sweetness of their youth just as he stripped off the ancient pine from their lands. Stumps and big bellies was all he left behind" (23–24). Mauser's conquest of Ojibwe women and their land, a small portion of the dispossession of vast tracts of Native American land across the United States, was analogous to sexual violence. The land was roughly captured, stripped, and sold, with no dignity in the transaction and solely for the pleasure of the purchaser. This is how Mauser came to speak Ojibwe, a proficiency shocking to Fleur, who is ostensibly unaware of the disturbing circumstances of his education in the tribal language. The colonizer must, to a degree, assimilate into the culture of the colonized in order to win trust and carry out his schemes.

Arguably Fleur's conquest of Mauser amounts to the same. By marrying him she knows that he is bound legally to her, and this ensures her reclamation of the Pillager land upon his death. Fleur's relationship with Mauser is one of master and servant, wherein Mauser is no longer the master in that equation. She is perfectly positioned to exact her murderous revenge, but an unplanned and difficult pregnancy delays her plan. Once their son, John James Mauser II, is born, her attention turns fully to her son's care as he suffers from an unidentified developmental condition, possibly fetal alcohol syndrome, as Fleur drank whiskey throughout the pregnancy. While the child heralds the final blow to Fleur's plans, her marriage, and the Mausers' financial situation, he also symbolizes the sins of the colonial past. He is the product not only of his parents' sins, Mauser's shady land dealings, and consequently Fleur's determined plans for revenge, but also many others ills that stem from colonialism. Fleur abandons her child Lulu to win back her ancestral land from the colonist who brought smallpox that killed her entire family, left her reproductive system damaged, and possibly caused her child's developmental difficulties; alcohol, the poison of her people and preferred bargaining tool of the colonizers, becomes her medication.

After Mauser is left in ruins, Fleur returns to the reservation, a "ghost of the girl" the community once knew, driving a white Cadillac, wearing spotless white attire, and carrying an impossibly white child (182). This white child, her son John James Mauser II, helps her win back her land, ironically since his own father is the one who stole it, stripped it, and sold it. The community rallies around Fleur as she wagers her Cadillac for the title of her land in a game of cards with the former Indian agent turned bar owner Jewett Parker Tatro and wins the game. The community accepts her return as the prodigal daughter and also a heroine of mythic proportions. Community and kinship are restored. Although she accomplished her mission against insurmountable odds, Fleur is left hollow; the elation from a hard-won victory is lacking. She is physically exhausted and spiritually damaged. Margaret performs a healing ritual, in which she administers love medicine to cleanse and restore Fleur and wash away her sins. Her victory does not heal all the wounds of dispossession; the harms of colonization still remain. Ultimately the value in Fleur's repossession of her ancestral land is in the hope it brings to the community and the inspirational tale it provides for future generations of the Ojibwe.

The Last Report of the Miracles at Little No Horse

If *Love Medicine* is the beginning of the epic, generating a number of storylines, then *The Last Report of the Miracles at Little No Horse* (2001) helps to develop further a number of story arcs and tie up some important loose ends. Erdrich accomplishes this while offering a rich portrait of one of her recurring characters, Father Damien Modeste, the culturally sensitive mission priest assigned to Little No Horse, the fictional reservation near the fictional town of Argus, North Dakota. The novel is a part epistolary and part historical account of the reservation and its inhabitants, particularly Sister Leopolda, known as Pauline Puyat before her conversion to Catholicism in *Tracks,* and Nanapush, Erdrich's inimitable, irreverent trickster character. The letters are in the form of the eponymous "report" from Father Damien to the Vatican. He directly addresses the Pope, though the specific pope in question changes as Father Damien reaches and surpasses the centenarian mark, outlasting the tenure of each pontiff. One of the dual purposes of Father Damien's reports is to discredit Sister Leopolda, who is under consideration for canonization. The reports collectively amount to a reverse hagiography of sorts, designed to critique rather than extol the virtues or honor the life and works of Sister Leopolda. The second purpose of Father Damien's reports is to offer a historical account of his own life in order to confess his own secrets and true identity in the hope of absolution. The main narrative, outside of the reports, augments the historical record through various discussions between Father Damien and Father Jude, the young priest appointed by the Vatican to investigate Sister Leopolda's life and rumored miracles.[9] Once again Erdrich uses storytelling to get to the essence of the truth—personal, local truth. Putting together the pieces of this novel with those in the entire Love Medicine series, readers arrive at a version of reality, albeit the storytellers' reality, which is the only way to come to any conclusions in Erdrich's fictional world. No monolithic factual narratives are proffered to readers; instead they are presented with a symphony of voices, which creates a picture of time, place, character, and history.[10]

While Erdrich's prevailing theme of storytelling infuses the novel, its primary concern is identity: male, female, Ojibwe, non-Ojibwe, Catholic, traditional, colonized, colonizer, saint, and sinner. More specifically the dissidence between self-identification and public persona is central. In this novel these crises of identity are evidenced most clearly in Father Damien, both ontologically and epistemologically. This mission priest, an instrument of colonization, instead finds himself deeply affected by his interactions with the Ojibwe. The souls Father Damien is meant to save, those of the Ojibwe, profoundly touch him: his mission, his way of life, his point of view, his spirituality, and ultimately his soul. Absorbed in learning the Ojibwe language, rituals, spiritual beliefs, and personal and public histories, Father Damien possesses an authentic desire to fuse his own shifting identity with one that he values as foundational and stable. While he sympathizes with various Ojibwe members of his Christian flock, more significantly he empathizes with those who have remained steadfast in traditional beliefs in the face of colonization and its attendant forced assimilation, particularly Nanapush. Metaphorically, then, Father Damien symbolizes the identity crisis of the Ojibwe in reverse; he undergoes a reverse assimilation.

Father Damien's openness to another way of being and knowing is at the heart of the novel. In part his sensitivity might be attributed to his long-held secret, revealed in his first report of the novel: he is actually a former nun named Sister Cecilia, who left the convent to pursue a secular life as Agnes DeWitt. Agnes was married to a man named Bernt Vogel, who was struck down and killed by an armed robber. Fleeing after this incident, Agnes is caught in a flood. She stumbles upon the body of a priest assigned to Little No Horse, who was en route to the reservation, according to his papers, when he perished in the flood. With no prospects for the future, she assumes the identity of the dead Father Damien and takes up his appointment as spiritual leader of the community in Little No Horse. The pressure of upholding both this sacred responsibility and her precarious deception is a constant source of anxiety for Agnes, now Father Damien. Not only does she feel the pull to assimilate culturally, but she must also alter her feminine identity to pass as a different gender. She imagines and tries to embody not only a priest's comportment but also the general attributes of a man. From her observations she creates a list, "Some Rules to Assist My Transformation," which includes "Make requests in the form of orders"; "Ask questions in the form of a statement"; "Advance no explanations"; "Admire women's handiwork with copious amazement"; and "Hum an occasional resolute march."[11] Armed with these rules, Agnes believes she can maintain her impersonation.

In light of Erdrich's typical trickster humor, Father Damien's ruse might not be fooling anyone on the reservation, though no one challenges him directly. Some think he is a two-spirit, a type of transgendered individual who wholly embodies both genders and is readily accepted in the Ojibwe community: "The priest was clearly not right, too womanly. Perhaps . . . here was a man like the famous Wishkob, the Sweet, who had seduced many other men and finally joined the family of a great war chief as a wife, where he had lived until old, well loved, as one of the women" (64). Others believe he is a homosexual, particularly when he falls in love and engages in a sexual relationship with a visiting priest, Father Gregory Wekkle. Curiously the mission nuns, who live and worship with him every day, appear oblivious to his masquerade, or they privately acknowledge the fact and relish this community of women in charge of their small outpost of the Catholic Church, which forbids women from leading the church as priests. Perhaps Erdrich has created a radical revenge fantasy played out by the nuns, who feel relegated to second-class status in the church, which adds a political dimension to the nuns' behavior though it is not explicitly stated in the text. Finally a number of individuals know he is a woman, including Nanapush, who glibly mentions it in conversation over a game of chess near the end of their decades-old friendship (230–32). A trickster always recognizes another trickster, and Nanapush pulls out this information at a key moment in the game, to gain an advantage on the chessboard by ruffling Father Damien. Like Nanapush, all in the community take Father Damien at face value, accepting whatever his biological actuality may technically be. Living on a boundary or in transition is the state of being for the Ojibwe on the reservation Father Damien calls home.

Metaphorically the two-spirit aspect of Father Damien is analogous to the identity crisis of the Ojibwe during colonialism and echoes Sister Leopolda's conversion in *Tracks*. Being pulled by two spirits, male and female, he must find a space in which he can exist. The circumstances of his physical, emotional, and spiritual survival dictate a need to merge his dueling aspects into one harmonious being in order to operate successfully in the world at large. Learning to live on the threshold, embodying two spirits, and adapting to a new world are likewise the keys to the success of the Ojibwe. Father Damien's position is even symbolic of Native American land itself, the site of many identity struggles, and the shifting boundaries imposed on it by the U.S. government. Father Damien's identity struggles offer freedom for him, however, as the similar struggles of Sister Leopolda, the mixed-blood convert Pauline, did for her. For Father Damien both gender roles fit, and his faith seamlessly fuses with Ojibwe spirituality. While being caught in a liminal space may be cause for frustration for many, it is in this space in which Father Damien thrives and becomes whole. He is wholly one individual, in a personal and spiritual sense, and culturally one with his community.

Where Erdrich offers a gentle portrait of transformation in Father Damien's reverse assimilation and relatively smooth integration of gender identities, her depiction of Lulu's forced enrollment in a residential government school exposes the lasting effects of colonization and assimilation on the Ojibwe. Though only a brief section of the novel, these pages mark the first time Erdrich describes Lulu's placement in boarding school and the cruelty she suffers at the hands of those in charge of her assimilation there. In many thematic ways, the episode is a long-form version of Erdrich's poem "Indian Boarding School: The Runaways." She illustrates yet another Ojibwe character's traumatization by the government school system. This childhood trauma is the chief cause of Lulu's rift with her mother, Fleur Pillager, which is presented in many of Erdrich's novels, from *Love Medicine* and *Tracks* to *The Bingo Palace* and *Four Souls.* Fleur's abandonment of Lulu in the pursuit of her single-minded revenge on John Mauser and mission to repossess her homeland, as dramatized in *Four Souls,* has an irrevocable and damning effect on their relationship. As Father Damien reports, "She had regained her land, but lost her daughter" (265). Fleur's abandonment of Lulu to the boarding school, for what she perceives as the greater good for her ancestry, is an insurmountable breach of trust. The sacred covenant between parent and child is broken. Fleur's violation of Lulu's utter faith and confidence in her as a mother, a child's first and only recourse, is analogous to the failed promise of fair and equitable treatment that the U.S. government made to the Ojibwe. In terms of emotional cost, the primal harm done by Fleur to Lulu's psyche is incalculable.

In her memories of the boarding school experience, the devastating turning point for Lulu is her dawning realization of what lies in store for her at the meeting place of the Ojibwe children and the school officials. Noting the neat line of the school's white "audoomobiig"—automobiles—Lulu sees "the children looking out through the windows, sad, vague, and indistinct as though gazing from underwater" (243). She implores Fleur to save her from this situation: "No! I tried to get my mother's attention. Let's go home, I said,

I want to go home. But my mother was staring at the people with the boards and the paper, and at the other Anishinaabeg gathered around them. Her face was neutral and heavy. A sickness of fear seized me. I tugged and pulled my mother's hand as if to bring it to life, but her hand was stiff, and cold, like the paw of a trapped, dead animal. And then she dragged me forward" (243). The flamboyant, unflappable, and fiercely independent Lulu Nanapush Lamartine of Erdrich's other novels is unrecognizable in the small, sensitive, affectionate, and sheltered child encountered in this childhood memory. Lulu reveals her emotional state upon reaching the boarding school confines:

> "Once I was alone it continued, the crying, for which I had no shame or remedy. It was a simple weeping in which the tears came up and flowered over. It wasn't painful and it wasn't unpleasant, this crying, it just was. *It just was and it just was,* I said once I became an adult woman known for never shedding tears. No, I never cried, not in love or in child-birth, not at death and not over any particular want or loss or piece of bad fortune. My tears had simply run out on that ride down to the school. That's when I came to know that to be left, sent off, abandoned, was not of the moment, but a black ditch to the side of the road of your life, a sudden washout, a pothole that went down to China" (244–45).

The insight Erdrich offers concerning Lulu's rough, insensitive exterior creates a new perspective by which to evaluate her character. The insensitive, promiscuous, defiant, and self-sufficient adult Lulu was forged out of the harsh reality of her childhood. Erdrich's inclusion of Lulu's story bears witness to the tens of thousands of children who faced the same fate during the "Indian" boarding school era.

Erdrich integrates Lulu's childhood story into the context of Father Damien's positive assimilation into Ojibwe society as a revealing counterpoint and an integral part of Ojibwe history on the reservation. His adoption of Ojibwe cultural and spiritual values is the focus of the novel. The hybrid Catholic-Ojibwe spirituality he practices both publicly and privately reveals Father Damien's innate respect for the traditional beliefs of his community, which cause no dissonance in his own Catholic belief system. To be sure "Father Damien had been converted by the good Nanapush. He now practiced a mixture of faiths, kept the pipe, translated hymns or brought in the drum, and had placed in the nave of his church a statue of the Virgin—solid, dark, kind eyed, hideous, and gentle. He was welcome where no other white man was allowed" (276). The ultimate testament to Father Damien's commitment to Ojibwe spirituality is revealed in the last moments of his life. His death and Nanapush's occur in the course of the novel. While their deaths bring to an end two remarkable lives, their stories remain for posterity. Erdrich offers hope through the lifelong relationship shared by these two characters. The relationship between a mission priest and a wily old Ojibwe trickster exemplifies true integration not only of life stories to pass down but also of two disparate cultures—Ojibwe and Euro-American, two improbably connected lives that have intertwined for decades with compassion, understanding, humor, mutual respect, and love. Father Damien and Nanapush are two sides of the same coin, embodying another kind of "two-spirit" sensibility; they are truly kindred spirits.

Nanapush's sensational death has mythic qualities, in keeping with his trickster nature. He lived a life guided by love, joy, and pleasure; his death is no exception. Done in by his wife's bad cooking and the resulting explosive flatulence, Nanapush succumbs—but only temporarily. He explains to Margaret: "I returned for one reason only, my wife. When I was gone and far away, I felt how you tried to revive me with the heat of your body. I was happy you tried to do that, my heart was full. This time when I left with harsh words on my lips about your cooking, I got a ways down the road leading to the spirit world, and I just couldn't go any farther, my dear woman, because I wronged you. I wanted to make things smooth between us. I came back to love you good" (295). Appropriately Nanapush's life story ends with a bang and not a whimper, so to speak, as he seduces Margaret one last time, assuring his place in Erdrich's Ojibwe folklore as one of her most revered, perceptive, witty, sagacious, oversexed, and, above all, loving characters. His legendary demise is filled with passion, humor, forgiveness, and love.

The death of Father Damien similarly leaves readers with a sense of Erdrich's affection for the character. Furthermore the respect the author holds for her own particular Ojibwe Catholicism, which blends both Catholic and traditional spiritual perspectives, is symbolized in Father Damien. In terms of assimilation, he exemplifies the ways in which the Ojibwe adapted to survive colonization and avoid extinction, by acknowledging and accepting another set of beliefs while preserving their Native spirituality. In describing Father Damien's final days, Erdrich refers to the character as the feminine Agnes. Dressed as the priest, Agnes rows to Spirit Island, the ancestral land of the Pillagers, with various supplies, including a case of wine, and instructions for her body to be "buried in the lake" (351). Dying and slightly afraid, she fondly recalls various parts of her life: all of the people who affected her, including Berndt Vogel, Mary Kashpaw, and Fleur Pillager. Agnes contemplates the change in her beliefs and values since living with the Ojibwe and learning their fascinating language, and her relationship with Nanapush: "Thank god, I met your visionary, strange servant Nanapush!" (349). Thinking on his adventures, Agnes develops uncontrollable spasms of laughter until she realizes, "I am going to laugh myself to death!" Nanapush gives Agnes a final, joyful gift: "It was then that she felt the stifled warm report of a blood vessel bursting just above her left ear" (349). At the moment of her death, a strong, reassuring hand carries her to the other side, the world of the spirits. Arguably the hand belongs to her dearest friend in life, Nanapush, though it could be that of her long-lost beloved husband, Berndt Vogel; her former lover, Father Gregory Wekkle; or her Christian savior, Jesus. Most likely the hand represents an amalgam of all of them. In the end Sister Leopolda's sinfulness and saintliness, the reason for the reports to the Vatican, are of little consequence. The story ultimately is about Father Damien and Agnes Dewitt, fused into one individual who finds eternal peace in the vestments of a priest, the passions of a woman, the soul of a believer, the openheartedness of a community, and the true and abiding spirit of Ojibwe friendship.

CHAPTER 4

The Plague of Doves and *The Round House*

Louise Erdrich has published other works that dramatize the historical and contemporary ramifications of colonization, including *The Plague of Doves* (2008) and *The Round House* (2012). An analysis of these two novels, along with a brief discussion of other selected works, is warranted to highlight their connections to the texts discussed in the previous chapters and to illustrate their valuable place in Erdrich's oeuvre, as they provide rich ground for various angles of investigation.[1] *The Beet Queen* (1986) and *The Master Butchers Singing Club* (2003), which both take place near the reservation in North Dakota, deal primarily with the experience of European, namely German, immigrants, inspired by Erdrich's paternal side of the family, particularly her grandfather Ludwig Erdrich and his wife, Mary Kroll. As early as the "Butcher's Wife" poems in *Jacklight,* Erdrich has been considering this part of her cultural heritage. The immigrant experience is analogous to the colonial experience in terms of identity and assimilation, but the perspective is a Euro-American one that reveals its own set of unique conflicts and consequences. Both *The Antelope Wife* (1998) and *Tales of Burning Love* (1996) are more closely aligned with the Love Medicine series: *The Antelope Wife* shares many of the thematic concerns of the series, while *Tales of Burning Love* features some of its characters and genealogical connections. *The Antelope Wife,* however, deals with two Ojibwe families living off-reservation in Minneapolis, with no easily discernable connection to the main clans of *Love Medicine.* While critical attention to the novel has considered its themes of history, assimilation, kinship, and oppression, an interesting and uninvestigated aspect, rich for bibliographic study, is Erdrich's revision of it, which was published in 2012. The editing choices Erdrich makes in the later version of the novel make it a work-in-progress and inform the reader of her commitment to the diligent revisioning of any "master story," offering open-ended, contestable versions for the reader's consideration.

Tales of Burning Love also acts as a revisioning, as it deals with John James Mauser III. The son of Mary Kashpaw and John James Mauser II, he is the product of an encounter described in *The Last Report on the Miracles at Little No Horse* and is Fleur Pillager's grandson. Referred to as Andy in the first chapter of *Love Medicine,* Mauser was with June Morrissey on the night of her death; in *Tales of Burning Love,* he recounts the episode from his perspective, offering a revision to that earlier tale. The novel also provides the end of Sister Leopolda's story, as her death occurs in the beginning. The death scene is poignant, and readers are confronted with a sympathetic version of Sister Leopolda not encountered in Erdrich's other novels. Dot Adare and Gerry Nanapush make appearances, as well, further developing their stories introduced in the Love Medicine series. Even with all of these connections, *Tales of Burning Love* centers around Mauser, so heavily assimilated that few are aware of his Ojibwe roots, and the various relationships with his ex-wives, who share with one another their tales of "burning love." The effects of colonization in the novel are peripheral and are represented symbolically in the form of Mauser's assimilation.

Shadow Tag (2010) is a departure for Erdrich, who characterizes it as a "suspense novel."[2] The novel deals primarily with the deterioration and ultimate demise of a married couple, as opposed to being a multigenerational, historical account of Ojibwe on the reservation. Storytelling is central, with the novel comprising two narratives: one contained in a red diary and one in a blue notebook. The main character, Irene America, keeps the story of her life in these two diametrically opposed documents once she realizes her husband, Gil, has betrayed her trust by regularly reading her diary. Erdrich saw *Shadow Tag* as a break from her signature storytelling style: "Writing from multiple points of view was a box for me, and I feel like with *Shadow Tag* I broke out of my box. . . . I was able to construct a narrative that went straight ahead, straight on, with a single narrator and a single point of view."[3] Relatively speaking, the narrative is more straightforward than in other of Erdrich's novels with multiple narrators. However the narrative strategy in *Shadow Tag* is consistent with Erdrich's characteristic narrative style, as it raises central questions of truth and reliability surrounding the dual narratives.

There are no connections of shared characters, places, or historical events between *Shadow Tag* and Erdrich's other novels. Even so the novel's themes of objectification and invisibility reveal a certain type of colonization: the artistic colonization of Native Americans. Through the symbolic use of mirrors, shadows, art, and the artist's gaze, Erdrich sets up a correlative between Gil, a painter, whose primary subject is his wife, Irene, an art historian, and the American painter George Catlin, whose nineteenth-century paintings of Native Americans established his fame as a portrait artist. Comparing the objectification of Irene in Gil's paintings to that of Native Americans by Catlin, Erdrich investigates, in her distinctive narrative style, the ways in which the artist's gaze and depictions of his subject robs that subject of power and voice. According to Gil, "Catlin absurdly . . . feared he could take their [Native Americans'] souls. . . . Gil himself could not bear to look at Catlin's work. The tragic irony of it offended him."[4] The real irony is Gil's own objectification of Irene in his paintings: in order to capture "the iconic suffering of her people" (37), he depicts her in humiliating poses.

Gil's portrayals of Irene "immediately evoked problems of exploitation, the indigenous body, the devouring momentum of history" (1). At first Irene sees no harm in posing for her husband's paintings: "The image is not the person . . . or even the shadow of a person. So how can a person be harmed by the depiction, even appropriation, of something as intangible as one's image?" (31). Increasingly through the novel, however, she realizes that Gil is in fact stealing some profound part of her being whenever he paints her. In one of the many disturbing examples of Gil's exploitation, he positions Irene with her legs spread apart as if she has drunkenly fallen asleep: "Gil stepped back, adjusted his lights to shine starkly between her legs. Her face was thrown into shadow" (162). Gil's objectification of Irene, his wife and mother of his children, is marked by an observer's distance and insensitivity, an impersonal and dehumanizing stance. Irene does come to recognize the risks of serving as Gil's subject: "By remaining still, in one position or another, for her husband, she had released a double into the world. It was impossible, now, to withdraw that reflection. Gil owned it. He had stepped on her shadow" (39). The narrator explains the connections between a person's soul and its representation in paintings, mirrors, and shadows: "A soul could be captured through a shadow. It was in the Ojibwe language. Waabaamoojichaagwaan—the word for mirror also can refer to shadow and to the soul: your soul is visible and can be seen. Gil had placed his foot on Irene's shadow when he painted her. And though she tried to pull away, it was impossible to tug that skein of darkness from under his heel" (40). Though *Shadow Tag* deals with aspects of artistic colonization, the focus of the novel is Irene's attempt to escape Gil's soul-stealing gaze and survive his marital and artistic oppression.

The Plague of Doves and *The Round House*

While many of Erdrich's novels feature recurring themes, interwoven families, and historically connected characters, *The Plague of Doves* and *The Round*

House are part of their own distinct series. As the first two parts of a planned trilogy, both novels explore the lasting effects of injustice on a community. Although they do share a few characters, and certainly stylistic elements and thematic concerns, with the Love Medicine series, *The Plague of Doves* and *The Round House* present interwoven characters haunted by a specific historical trauma. The plight of the Ojibwe, and all Native Americans, to overcome the debilitating and deadly racism prevalent in the communities that border reservations becomes painfully clear in *The Plague of Doves,* when three Ojibwe, two men and a boy, are lynched in the small fictional border town of Pluto, North Dakota, for a crime they did not commit. The crime is the murder of a local farming family, the Lochrens, whose bodies are discovered by the Ojibwe men. Erdrich's story recalls the historical lynching of three Dakota men by a mob in 1897 in retribution for the killing of a farm family of six—four generations, including twin infant sons and their aged great-grandmother—in North Dakota.[5] The central event of the novel is based on a devastating episode in Native American history when "in the heat of things, a group of men ran down a party of Indians and what occurred was a shameful piece of what was called at the time 'rough justice.'"[6] Erdrich explains: "The book revolves or spins off of a lynching of Native Americans—Native American men, young men. One boy was only thirteen years old. This particular incident, which occurred in 1897, haunted me. It really happened. I didn't know how I was going to get to it, and so I wrote around it for many years and put together differing stories. . . . My mother is Ojibwa, Turtle Mountain Ojibwa. My father is non-Indian. And this book talks about what it's like for a community to come to terms with the lack of justice. There was never any justice done. This was an act of vengeance that reverberates throughout the whole community for generations."[7] Erdrich's fictionalized version involves the lynching of three men in 1911: Cuthbert Peace, the medicine man Asiginak, and Holy Track, Asiginak's young nephew, who are captured by a mob of townsfolk and hanged to death from a large oak tree. The lynching has a rippling effect through the community and through time, connecting various Ojibwe and non-Ojibwe characters: "Now that some of us have mixed in the spring of our existence both guilt and victim, there is no unraveling of the rope" (243). As in other Erdrich novels, the inhabitants in and around the reservation are inextricably linked by circumstance and blood.

Soon after becoming a finalist for the Pulitzer Prize, *The Plague of Doves* began to garner critical attention, with the scholarship focused on the abiding themes of Erdrich's work: narrative style, historical trauma, cultural identity, storytelling, and the interconnectedness of a community. Erdrich employs multiple narrators to tell the story of Pluto's formation, turbulent history, and present social and economic conditions. Through Evelina Harp, a mixed-blood adolescent; Judge Bazil Coutts, a mixed-blood resident with ties to the town's founders and to the inimitable Nanapush; Marn Wolde, a woman from a local farming family; and Cordelia Lochren, a local physician and sole survivor of the Lochren farm murders, Erdrich pieces together the story of the lynching, documents Pluto's history, and reveals the true identity of the Lochrens' murderer. Harp and Coutts narrate the majority of the novel, with Wolde and Lochren each narrating a single section. Arguably the primary narrator is Evelina Harp, who questions various members of the community both on and off the reservation to cobble together an understanding of her family history and her grandfather Mooshum's escape from the lynching—four men were hanged that day, and one miraculously walked away with his life. Evelina reveals private struggles with identity issues, particularly her cultural and sexual identity, through the course of her narration as well.

Evelina's narration recounts her early life, the colorful (and off-color) childhood stories of her grandfather, and certain memorable experiences—childhood injustices, romantic involvements, frustrations, and passions—from her school days to burgeoning adulthood. Mooshum's story of the lynching captures her imagination and moves her to investigate the history of the original families of the town and their descendants: "The story Mooshum told us had its repercussions—the first being that I could not look at anyone in quite the same way anymore. I became obsessed with lineage. . . . I wrote down as much of Mooshum's story as I could remember, and then the relatives of everyone I knew—parents, grandparents, way on back in time. I traced the blood history of the murders through my classmates and friends until I could draw out elaborate spider webs of lines and intersecting circles" (86). Evelina's narrow sense of community widens as she traces the connections, past and present, among Ojibwe and non-Ojibwe. Erdrich creates an intricate web of connections, blurring the lines that separate individuals in Evelina's world, creating a new awareness of cultural identity for her as a mixed-blood Ojibwe. Where the blame for the lynching rested solely with the townspeople, the white mob, Evelina uncovers her own family's portion of culpability for the horrific, haunting event. As a result of her tireless investigation, she discovers the prime mover of events—her own beloved Mooshum.

In his depiction of events, Mooshum leaves out vital information, a common occurrence in historical tales or eyewitness testimony. In Mooshum's case shame and guilt rather than loss of memory account for his omissions. Peace, Asiginak, Holy Track, and Mooshum unwittingly stumbled upon the slaughtered Lochren family. Had the group moved on instead of stopping to rescue the lone survivor, a starving infant, they might have avoided the lynching. Mooshum, in a drunken stupor, reveals the incident to his wife Junesse's estranged father, Eugene Wildstrand, who appoints himself leader of the vigilante mob that forms after the murders. Mooshum's actions warrant blame only for his lack of discretion and foresight. The townsfolk likely would have indicted another group of Ojibwe men for the murders if not them, especially in the absence of legitimate suspects. While the specter of colonization in Erdrich's work is sometimes abstract and indirect, the real, everyday racism rampant in American towns, particularly those bordering reservations in the early twentieth century, is brought into sharp focus in the story of the lynching.

The egregiousness of the act, the mob's utter disregard for truth and lawful justice, is most evident in the killing of Holy Track. In most civilized societies, the execution of a minor would not be considered except in the most heinous cases and with judicious consideration, which makes the rush to judgment in Holy Track's case unfathomable. It is the doubt over his innocence in the heart of Father Severine, his mentor at the parish church, that seems most treacherous to Holy Track, however. As a young child, Holy Track's dying mother had crosses affixed to the rubber soles of his boots to protect him from sickness. Indeed he did not succumb to smallpox or tuberculosis as did so many Ojibwe in the turn of the last century, but his mother was unable to inoculate him against the sickness of racism.

Under the care and teaching of Father Severine, Holy Track became a member of the church and a promising understudy; the priest "very much loved the boy Holy Track" (65). Severine does offer him sanctuary, though a reluctant one, in his time of greatest need, as he runs from the gathering lynch mob. When he arrives at the door of the church, he is greeted with skepticism: "The priest's face worked back and for the between expressions of pity and disgust, and at last settled on peevish disappointment. 'I suppose you are here to confess.' His voice was shaky and shrill. His breath was agitated. 'You have done a monstrous thing!' He seemed to gather himself and stepped backwards" (67). Severine's stepping away from Holy Track is both a literal and symbolic movement. The retreat signals his doubt and lack of faith in the boy, though Holy Track is as close as a son to him. Despite his obvious fatherly affection, Severine is quick to pass judgment, exposing a simmering disappointment existing near the surface of his opinion of Holy Track. The inherent prejudice toward the Ojibwe is painfully evident in this moment. As a representative of the Catholic Church, Severine should be espousing love and faith as the abiding principles dictating his actions. Instead suspicion and misgiving characterize his response. He readily assumes Holy Track's guilt and eschewal of Catholic values and mores. In his sacrifice Holy Track achieves a kind of sainthood. If not in the Catholic Church, then in the Ojibwe community, he becomes an emblem of love and faith. The lynch mob fails to recognize the real perpetrator of the crime and protect the community from a killer; it also, in exacting its irreversible, unholy punishment, brutally ushers Peace, Asiginak, and Holy Track into the realm of martyrdom. The lynching becomes part of the fabric of the community, both Ojibwe and non-Ojibwe, for generations to come.

The other major narrator in *The Plague of Doves,* Judge Antoine Bazil Coutts, provides further insights into the profound interrelationship of history, injustice, and the law weighing heavily on this community and, specifically, on his character in both this novel and *The Round House.* In *The Plague of Doves,* Coutts presents a personal history of his ancestry and his connections to the victims and the perpetrators of the lynching. He also recounts the development of his relationship with his wife, Geraldine Milk, daughter of tribal elder Seraph Milk, lovingly referred to as Mooshum, or "Grandfather," by all. Most significant, Coutts's narration sheds light on the legal wrangling of the tribe with the federal government and the compelling inspiration for his vocation as tribal judge. As he describes it, "I am sentenced to keep watch over this small patch of earth, to judge its miseries and tell its stories" (217).

The small patch of earth where Coutts presides, the setting for both *The Plague of Doves* and *The Round House,* is Erdrich's fictional North Dakota reservation, which is bordered by the three towns of Hoopdance, Argus, and Pluto, where the lynching occurred. The judge is the product of a long line of residents, both Ojibwe and non-Ojibwe, whose intermarriages have instilled in him a profound sense of identification with both parts of his cultural heritage. This mixed-blood status allows him to "know something about both sides of many cases" he hears in his courtroom (114). In addition to marrying Ojibwe women, both Coutts's father and grandfather were lawyers, giving them tribal membership and legal authority in the Ojibwe community, "an unusual combination . . . but increasingly handy as tribal law and the complication of federal versus state jurisdiction were just beginning to become manifest" (115). Coutts follows his paternal legacy, marries Geraldine, an Ojibwe woman, and achieves the position of tribal judge on the reservation. As tribal judge he uses the position to "maintain the sovereignty of tribal law on tribal land" (115). Early on Coutts is aware of the importance of his position and the struggles he will face defending the legal rights of the tribe, whose sovereignty is under constant attack. As a young man, he accompanies his father, the only lawyer from the community, on a trip to Washington "to fight a policy that would have terminated our relationship with the United States government guarantee by treaty" (92). The informal education he receives through observing the legal efforts of his family to protect the rights of the Ojibwe combines with his schooling to create a measured, intellectual quality of character in Coutts. Even with all of this legal preparation, however, justice remains sadly elusive, and the law fails

Coutts and his family, adding even more pain and frustration to an already agonizing situation, as Erdrich depicts in *The Round House.* In that novel Judge Coutts finds his faith in the law profoundly tested.

The lasting contemporary consequences of settlement and colonialism, in the form of unjust yet binding federal laws, are the focus of *The Round House.* Particularly the plight of the Ojibwe to practice self-determination in the face of blurred boundaries and the sometimes overlapping jurisdictions of tribal, state, and federal law emphasizes the lack of sovereignty or self-rule of Native Americans. As always in Erdrich's fiction, the past shapes the present and informs the future. Through communal storytelling and historical memory, characters must decide how to process past events in order to proceed into the future, not by forgetting but by remembering, acknowledging, learning, and healing. Accordingly the memory of the lynch mob haunts the characters of *The Round House,* who live on the same North Dakota reservation near Pluto. Though the characters in this novel must contend with a horrific act inflicted upon a respected family in their present day, the late 1980s, "it's all about healing in the end," explained Erdrich in 2012.[8]

The Round House shares with *The Plague of Doves* many of the same characters or their descendants: Coutts, Geraldine, Mooshum, Clemence, and Peace. Ever present in the novels as well is the memory of Nanapush. *The Round House* also shares thematic concerns, particularly the theme of justice, which becomes the central focus of this novel. The most notable difference between the two novels, however, is the narrative style. *The Round House* is told in first person, as opposed to multiple narrators alternating with third-person narration. The novel is the closest to a mainstream narrative found in any of Erdrich's adult fiction, with little of her experimental style. The events of the novel are viewed from the perspective of thirteen-year-old Joe Coutts, the son of Judge Coutts and Geraldine. Erdrich chooses this point of view to represent Joe's lack of agency in the face of the devastating sexual assault suffered by his mother. Joe's position is analogous to that of the Ojibwe tribe; both are stymied in their bids for justice and are too easily trumped by a greater authority, namely federal law. The laws of the land—not the Native Americans' but the U.S. government's—bind Native peoples and render them powerless to exact justice on perpetrators from the greater U.S. population, who are protected by federal law. Joe's position is powerless; things happen to him. Erdrich's narrative choice is also emblematic of her intention to get across an explicit political message that demands a clear narrative style: that contemporary Ojibwe communities still suffer the disenfranchisement of the colonized. She explained her desire to focus on an "instance of injustice" in the novel and expose the lived reality of tribal communities: "The long history of injustice in a community has enormous repercussions for how people function as a whole. And when people believe there is no justice to be attained, they behave in ways that are either defeated or vengeful."[9] The story of the novel is the story of this injustice and the devastating consequences of the powerlessness felt by the Coutts family.

In an op-ed piece for the *New York Times,* Erdrich enumerated some alarming statistics about sexual violence toward Native American women: "The Justice Department reports that one in three Native women is raped over her lifetime, while other sources report that many Native women are too demoralized to report rape. Perhaps this is because federal prosecutors decline to prosecute 67 percent of sexual abuse cases, according to the Government Accountability Office. . . . More than 80 percent of sex crimes on reservations are committed by non-Indian men, who are immune from prosecution by tribal courts."[10] Erdrich argued that tribal courts must be granted jurisdiction to prosecute these crimes against tribal members: "To protect Native women, tribal authorities must be able to apprehend, charge and try rapists—regardless of race. Tribal courts had such jurisdiction until 1978, when the Supreme Court ruled that they did not have inherent jurisdiction to try non-Indians without specific authorization from Congress."[11] Without the means to apprehend and punish non-Native sexual criminals, the reservation becomes a lawless site for potential victimizers, from within the reservation and from its surrounding communities. Justice and retribution for a violent sex crime is often, as a consequence of the law, out of reach for Native American families. This untenable and challenging position is the key problem dramatized in *The Round House.*

As is often the case with rape, Geraldine's assault has to do as much with power as with brutal sexual violence. The perpetrator, Linden Lark, is a non-Native member of the surrounding community and carries out his assault with impunity, as the tribal courts are powerless to prosecute him. Geraldine recalls Lark's taunts after the rape: "'I suppose I am one of those people who just hates Indians generally and especially for they were at odds with my folks way back but especially my feeling is that Indian women are'—what he called us, I don't want to say."[12] The combination of Lark's evident racism, his feeling of superiority, and the knowledge of his rights as a non-Native arms him with a dangerous self-confidence: "He said we have no standing under the law for a good reason and yet have continued to diminish the white man and to take his honor. . . . I won't get caught, he said. I've been boning up on law. . . . I know as much law as a judge. Know any judges? I have no fear. Things are the wrong way around, he said. But here in this place I make things the right way around for me. The strong should rule the weak. Instead of the weak the strong! It is the weak who pull down the strong. But I won't get caught" (161). Not simply a desire for sex but also a sense of racial and cultural omnipotence drives Lark.

The dominance he feels over Geraldine provides a rush of pleasure and feelings of satisfaction, the direct converse of the helplessness and disorientation she feels. She cannot recall where exactly the rape took place, though she knows it happened somewhere on the land surrounding the tribal round house, which is where she listens to Lark's ranting. The uncertainty about location is at the heart of the problem. Judge Coutts presses Geraldine to recall details, though she was hooded and bound, since "three classes of land meet there" in the area abutting the round house (160). The essential question of whether the crime occurred on tribal, state, or federal land determines jurisdictional prerogative. Immersed in her suffering and incapacitated by physical, emotional, and spiritual damage, Geraldine cannot provide a definitive answer.

The only thing she knows with certainty is that Lark intended to kill her by burning her alive in the round house had she not escaped. By physically and psychologically torturing her there, he intended to denigrate the entire Ojibwe community. Symbolizing a cultural as well as physical violation, his actions constitute a hate crime. The desecration of the round house, a communal and sacred space, is akin to defacing any other building of worship or cultural gathering place. The purpose of the round house is to offer a safe space for traditional spiritual ceremonies, "during the old days when Indians could not practice their religion—well, actually not such old days: pre-1978" (59). Not until 1978 did Congress pass the American Indian Religious Freedom Act, allowing Native Americans to practice their traditional beliefs openly. The community "pretended" the round house was a "social dance hall or brought their Bibles for gatherings" (60), just in case any government or Christian authorities stopped in to check. At the first sign of a non-Native person, the "water drums and eagle feathers and the medicine bags and birchbark scrolls and sacred pipes were in a couple of motorboats halfway across the lake" (60). The round house, then, is emblematic in two significant ways: its function in the community and its position near three distinct jurisdictional lands.

Tribal law has its boundaries, which leaves Joe and his family frustrated in their search for justice. The difficulty of finding justice on Native American reservations is due to the intersection of jurisdictions. In a 2012 NPR interview, Erdrich explained that "there are several kinds of land on reservations. And all of these pieces of land have different entities that are in charge of enforcing laws on this land. So in this case, Geraldine Coutts does not know where her attacker raped her. She didn't see, she doesn't know. . . . It is very, very difficult to find justice because there's no clear entity who is in charge of seeking justice for her."[13] The overwhelming force the federal law exerts on tribal law is analogous to the oppressive nature of rape. Erdrich pays keen attention throughout the novel to a number of historical cases involving and contributing to the oppression of Native Americans. Joe pores over federal and tribal cases to learn the origins of his family's present predicament. His father explains that the most irksome aspect of the law is the enduring acceptance of the archaic language used in historical judicial opinions, specifically Chief Justice John Marshall's, that still survives: "We were savages living off the forest, and to leave our land to us was to leave it useless wilderness, that our character and religion is of so inferior a stamp that the superior genius of Europe must certainly claim ascendancy" (229). The judge identifies for Joe the case that dealt a crippling blow to the safety and the sovereignty of the Ojibwe. *Oliphant v. Suquamish* is the decision that "took from us the right to prosecute non-Indians who commit crimes on our land" (229). Joe is shocked by his father's capitulation to federal law and abiding commitment to staying within the bounds of his tribal authority. The current law provides no legal recourse or relief for the Coutts family, and Joe is confounded by the judge's seeming lack of passion. He does not see that rash action is the providence of the young and naive and that the tribal elders must see beyond the devastating present and into the possibilities of the future. The elder Coutts explains that "we are trying to build a solid base here for our sovereignty. We try to press against the boundaries of what we are allowed, walk a step past the edge. Our records will be scrutinized by Congress one day and decision on whether to enlarge our jurisdiction will be made. Some day" (230). Coutts has faith in the law and a belief that if he runs a tight courtroom where he takes no liberties with his position and follows the letter of the law, perhaps his diligence will impress the U.S. government and be rewarded in the form of revised laws for future generations of Ojibwe. Coutts imagines himself as "the hanging judge in an old western," but "beyond playing cowboy" (196) in his imagination, he has a practical goal in mind with real-world implications: "We want to the right to prosecute criminals of all races on all within our original boundaries" (230–31). Coutts wisely seeks his own tempered counsel, but an impassioned Joe is not satisfied or impressed by his father's measured response to the situation.

Contrary to Joe's opinion of him, Coutts is not dispassionate and unaffected, nor should his temperance be mistaken for weakness; he is in an impossible situation, both legally and personally. Responsible for the well-being of his wife and son, he must reconcile his faith in the law with an overwhelming desire to defend his family by any means. Serving as a tribal judge compels him to act according to the legal imperative; he must master his anger and need for vengeance in order to uphold the central obligation he bears to the tribal community as their judicial representative. A misstep on his part could result in lasting and deleterious consequences for the entire Ojibwe community. Erdrich masterfully exemplifies Coutts's untenable internal conflict and merges it with the ways in which the attack on Geraldine impacts the everyday lives of his family. A seemingly innocuous visit to the grocery store turns into a pivotal moment for Coutts and Joe, who are running errands for the convalescing Geraldine. While searching for household items on the grocery list, trying to maintain a semblance of normalcy and domesticity, they confront a gloating Linden Lark: "There was a moment where all we did was stare. Then motion. My father threw the cream, surged forward, and grabbed Lark by the shoulders. He spun Lark, jamming him backward, then gripped Lark around the throat with both hands. . . . He attacked with such an instinct of sudden rage it looked slick as a movie stunt" (243–44). Running into his wife's rapist at the grocery store is too much for Coutts; the encounter is another kind of attack on the family. His identification with the law is tested; his identity as husband and father wins out, and he surrenders to his rage. Joe is momentarily impressed, until his father collapses from a heart attack in front of a smiling Lark, who seems pleased by the attack. Erdrich explained in a 2012 interview that "aside from the rapes themselves, there are so many terrible things about what happens in these situations, including the resignation that the women feel when everyone knows that the perpetrator is guilty and people even see the perpetrator all the time, and when the woman who's suffered at that person's hands is confronted by that person in her daily life. There's also the tragic falling apart of families when someone is raped and there is no justice."[14] Living with the ever-present possibility of running into Geraldine's rapist, the Coutts family faces a maddening predicament in the community. As long as Lark evades justice, they cannot begin the process of mental, emotional, and spiritual healing they all desperately need.

Erdrich understands that when the perpetrator of the crime, the one who should carry the weight of culpability and shame, is not held accountable, the family who suffers the injustice takes on the burden of guilt and blame and divides it among themselves. Joe sees this happening and struggles to understand his father's unwavering faith in a broken legal system. In some measure Joe interprets Coutts's enfeebling heart attack as frailty emblematic of the failure of the federal and tribal law to protect his people and avenge crimes against them. By rendering tribal law impotent with respect to the prosecution of non-Natives, the federal government effectively justifies vigilantism in Joe's eyes, which is what he resorts to. Killing Lark with the aid of his steady-handed friend Cappy, he justifies committing the crime so that another crime does not go unpunished. Erdrich has said that Joe's actions, though misguided, are understandable: "In writing the book, the question was: If a tribal judge—someone who has spent his life in the law—cannot find justice for the woman he loves, where is justice? And the book is also about the legacy of generations of injustice, and what comes of that. Because, of course, what comes of that is an individual needs to seek justice in their own way when they can't find justice through the system. And that brings chaos."[15] For Joe a little chaos seems in order. He is well aware of the history of injustice on the reservation. As he drives by the "hanging tree," the oak that was used in the lynching of Cuthbert Peace, Asiginak, and Holy Track, he notes the memorial prayer flags surrounding the base of the tree and the exasperating reality of historical injustice in the community: "None of the killers ever went on trial" for the crime committed at the site. Joe also knows that Lark's great-uncle was part of the lynching party, adding fuel to his fire for vengeance. The rough justice of *The Plague of Doves* strikes the community again in the form of Lark's killing. This time, however, Joe believes he has set right the sins of the past in his act of retribution: "It was no lynching. There was no question of his guilt. . . . Lark's killing is a wrong thing that serves an ideal justice. It settles a legal enigma. It threads that unfair maze of land title law by which Lark could not be prosecuted. His death was the exit" (306). In other words Lark's death was a compelling escape route out of the impossible legal conundrum facing Joe and his family. The death also exacts a measure of reckoning for the members of the lynch mob who served as judge and jury for the three Ojibwe men in 1911. Erdrich's characters never elude the reach of the past and the demands of history.

The consequence of colonialism, the fragmentation of the land, results in impersonal boundaries, liminal spaces. Home should not be a boundary but a place of security and protection. The murder of Lark provides some of the relief that Joe anticipates, but he knows that rough justice is no way to exact justice in a lawful community. With that deep, personal truth, he follows in the footsteps of his paternal side of the family and becomes a lawyer, working within the system to enact change. In that sense the lessons of history have impressed upon him the need for an activist stance in his legal practice. The future may find Joe entering politics or government; the possibilities and opportunities for action are endless. On the other hand, he may follow in his father's stoic footsteps and be content with doing his part locally. The reservation sees its share of pain and will someday need a new tribal judge. Joe may come to realize, in the fullness of time, what Coutts already understands inherently, as he quotes Marcus Aurelius: "Very little is needed to make a happy life" (35).

CHAPTER 5

The Birchbark House Series

In any study of Louise Erdrich that takes into account the colonial themes of her oeuvre, the books she has written for children provide a valuable, first-order understanding of Ojibwe life before the onslaught of settlement. Her first two publications exclusively for children, the picture books *Grandmother's Pigeon* (1996) and *The Range Eternal* (2002), are short-form examples of what becomes fully developed in the Birchbark House series. In these later books, Erdrich provides a precontact setting and an indispensable depiction of everyday Anishinaabe life untouched by colonization. This portrait of precolonial life serves as a testament to the firmly established traditions and culture of the Anishinaabe. In Erdrich's adult fiction, the history of colonization is told in flashbacks, in stories of the old ways, and in myths passed down by tribal elders. The books in the Birchbark House series, by contrast, stand as a powerful testament to the old ways. The reader gets a genuine sense of the daily life, through the seasons, of a typical Ojibwe clan and community. At the same time, a sense of loss pervades these books. The slow burn of Euro-American settlement begins in the second book, *The Range Eternal,* and grows to an inexorable inferno by the last published book in the series, *Chickadee* (2012).

The colonization of Native American land was a three-pronged attack: the tribal population was ravaged by communicable disease in the various forms of smallpox, typhoid, tuberculosis, and influenza; was assaulted culturally through language, religion, and Western customs; and was subjugated by the U.S. government with its attendant politics, bureaucracy, laws, and policies. The indigenous population of the land today called the United States was divided into numerous tribes and clans, with unique languages, systems of government, social laws, and traditions. While many of the Native people faced the same concerns over colonization, Erdrich's work focuses on the Ojibwe tribe, which made Minnesota its home until westward expansion forced tribal peoples west, primarily into North Dakota. With their reliance on the land, the Ojibwe, along with many of the tribes in North America, faced extinction as the encroaching settlers acquired land parcel by parcel through manipulative land transactions, various governmental laws and policies, and force. The survival of many tribes was dependent on the use of land for sustenance. With the loss of that land, the tribal way of life was changed from a hunting and gathering existence to a capitalistic one. While so much Native American literature focuses on the victimization of tribes, the prevailing theme in the Birchbark House series is survival and healing. Forgetting is not the way to healing; rather remembering the past, analyzing its effects on the present, learning its lessons, and avoiding historical traps and pitfalls allow future generations to move on successfully. Knowledge is power. Like Scheherazade in *The Arabian Nights,* Erdrich understands that storytelling is survival.

In the time period covered in the Birchbark House series, treaties secured the lands and the way of life of the Ojibwe in the Midwest. In historical terms the relatively new U.S. government had only begun its aggressive push west, and consequently Erdrich presents a picture of life untouched on the continuum of colonization. Often the history books read by U.S. schoolchildren, TV westerns such as *The Long Ranger,* and many John Wayne movies present caricatures of Indians. Whether in the context of Columbus's "discovery" of the New World, the first Thanksgiving, or the early settlements of Plymouth and Jamestown, Native Americans are depicted as exotic ornamentation, helpful tour guides, and cunning savages. They speak no formal indigenous language, emitting only grunts, war cries, and other guttural utterances. Erdrich's series offers a corrective to this stereotype by creating three-dimensional portraits with all the attendant emotions, desires, hopes, ambitions, fears, crises, resolutions, relationships, and everyday experiences. The themes of identity, its connection to the land, and the power of storytelling, and the rich cultural traditions found in her adult fiction, grow from seeds planted in these depictions of earlier times. Through storytelling Erdrich weaves Ojibwe history, mythology, spirituality, tradition, and culture through the ongoing story of Omakayas, the protagonist of the series.

As with other storytellers throughout Ojibwe history, Erdrich continues the art of preserving culture through the transmittal of communal and personal stories. This series offers monumental learning moments not often found in her adult fiction. For example Erdrich's use of the Ojibwe language offers a way of understanding it not offered in the adult fiction. She not only offers context clues and parenthetical references when using Ojibwe words but also provides a glossary so that the meanings are made abundantly clear. Thus she keeps the language alive by introducing it to both Native and non-Native readers. Since Ojibwe is an oral language, Erdrich provides a phonetic guide as to how the words are said aloud. Erdrich offers the examples of the language not only as a teaching strategy but also as a way of preserving a vital aspect of Ojibwe culture. Every person who says a name or a word in Ojibwe is keeping the culture alive.

Scholarship on the Birchbark House series has posited that it is a response to and revision of Laura Ingalls Wilder's Little House on the Prairie books.[1] While this assertion has merit, placing the series in the context of the western frontier narrative is itself a form of literary colonization, even if the Erdrich's books are a perceived as a reaction to Wilder's non–Native American perspective of settlement. For Wilder the "frontier" was a novel, exotic, dangerous, and adventurous place; however for the characters of the Birchbark House series, the wild frontier described in Wilder's books is home. Erdrich has explained her relationship to Wilder's series this way: "I read them as a child, and in rereading them as an adult, I was shocked to recognize that not only was there no consciousness about the displaced people whose land the newcomers were taking but also that there was a fair amount of racism. In the Little House books there are always these moves from place to place. The fact is that any time land was opening up, it was land from which native people were displaced, and in every Ojibwa family there's a similar series of moves."[2] The tribal ways of life, values and attitudes, and traditions tied to community and the land, as well the Native relationship with the natural world and communion with the spiritual world, are explored and described in the series. Readers get a real sense of what has been lost, as opposed to what has been "discovered" by westerners. The trauma of encroaching settlement and Western ways of being signaled a real existential crisis among the Ojibwe. In that context the land is a familiar, life-sustaining habitat deeply integrated into the lives of Omakayas and her community. Consequently it would be more appropriate to look at the Birchbark House series as a corrective prequel to the Little House series: Erdrich is not revising the account of the frontier of popular Western imagination; she is presenting the lived history of an indigenous people.

The Birchbark House series is a multipart epic, spanning one hundred years of an Ojibwe clan, starting with the origin and life of the main character, Omakayas, and continuing with her descendants.[3] The first book, *The Birchbark House* (1999), a finalist for a National Book Award, begins in roughly 1840 and immediately jumps to 1847. The second book, *The Game of Silence* (2005), picks up Omakayas's story when she is ten years old, in 1850. The next novel, *The Porcupine Year* (2008), follows a year in Omakayas's life in 1852. The fourth novel, *Chickadee,* winner of the 2013 Scott O'Dell Award for Historical Fiction, forwards the action some fourteen years to the year 1866.

The Birchbark House

The Birchbark House depicts what the Ojibwes lost in terms of land and all that is tied to it. The lives of the characters are dictated by nature and the landscape: the seasons, the wildlife, the plants, the lakes and rivers, the weather. Precontact life is mostly intact for the group of Ojibwe introduced in the book, though colonization has been an ongoing situation for more than a century by the timeline of the story. In the Midwest bands of Ojibwe were sustaining their ways of life since treaties had been signed to protect the land and its people. The idea of leaving and starting anew is a remote nightmare to Omakayas and her family.

In the acknowledgments of *The Birchbark House,* Erdrich offers a brief personal history.[4] She explains that the name *Omakayas* appears on a Turtle Mountain census form from 1892. She asks the reader to use the correct Ojibwe pronunciation and to "speak this name out loud" in order to honor "the life of an Ojibwa girl who lived long ago." She further explains that the book is "an attempt to retrace my own family's history," revealing that both sides of her family lived on Madeline Island during the time in which the book is set. The acknowledgments affirm Erdrich's belief in the vital potential of storytelling. Even though the book and the series that follows are commonly referred to as historical fiction, Erdrich is actually engaged in writing a fictionalized history.[5] While this may seem like a purely semantic distinction, the re-creation of history, a very personal history, is based on the lived experience of a people and the stories they have passed down for generations. Historical fiction is a separate genre; its primary focus is to capture a historical period, not a living story. For the Ojibwe traditions, spiritual beliefs, cultural attitudes, ways of interacting with nature, everyday life, crisis management, healing, and tribal history are passed through storytelling. In this way *The Birchbark House* is not storytelling for its own sake but is an effort to keep alive the rich history of the Ojibwe. Many traditional elements of Ojibwe life are still practiced today because of storytelling. Most aspects of everyday life are touched upon during the course of the book. It is, in short, a lesson in Ojibwe life and culture.

Another key feature of the series is the use of the Ojibwe language. Through these books Erdrich is giving readers an introductory lesson in Ojibwe. By including a glossary of terms with phonetic pronunciations at the end of the book and providing context clues or parenthetical translations throughout the text, Erdrich preserves and records the language. Though Ojibwe is an oral language and Erdrich's medium is the written word, transcribing it is an important step in recording it for generations to come. Ostensibly Erdrich is translating the Ojibwe conversations of the characters into English; therefore the cadence, rhythms, idiomatic expressions, humor, and vitality of the language must be approximated in English throughout the novels. Faced with the difficulty of transcribing an oral language, Erdrich offers a rudimentary Ojibwe to her readers and finds English correlatives to the Ojibwe dialogue. While her translations may be elementary, her commitment to using the language means that the series is not just the story of an Ojibwe girl but also a history of a language and culture that has faced extinction and survived. Colonization happens in language as much as it happens elsewhere. By privileging English the Euro-American colonists intended to extinguish the language of indigenous peoples if not the speakers themselves. So much of the history and identity of a people is tied up with their native language, and colonists recognized that killing the language was a strategy for killing the culture. Obviously the language was used for communication, but that communication was vital to the survival of Ojibwe culture as well. Naming ceremonies, healing songs, and teaching stories were all conveyed in the language: the names have meanings, the songs are personal mantras, and the stories are part of the healing process. Language is inextricably tied to history and place for the Ojibwe; losing it could have devastating consequences.

In addition to its linguistic offerings, *The Birchbark House* is a record of the lives of a group of Ojibwe in the mid-1800s who lived "at the edge of the village of La Pointe, on an island in Lake Superior . . . called Moningwanaykaning, Island of the Golden-Breasted Woodpecker" (6). Erdrich explains that this island, also referred to as Madeline Island, is the "spiritual home of the Anishinaabeg" (243). The story follows a year, 1847, in the life of Omakayas, "Little Frog," and her adoptive family. As the prologue to the novel explains, passing fur traders discovered Omakayas alone on nearby Spirit Island, surrounded by her deceased relatives. Her biological family was devastated by smallpox, one of the many diseases of European origin that indigenous populations fell victim to during colonization. Smallpox historically wiped out entire clans and communities, as Erdrich portrays in her adult fiction. As Erdrich remarked in a 1999 interview, "Smallpox just wiped out 9 of 10 people. . . . It's such an inconceivable horror. And it's so undocumented by native people because everything comes down orally. But my mother remembers people who did survive with smallpox scars up to the turn of the century. I wanted to start the book with a kind of mystery but also show that the people who survived were just a very tiny percentage. That is still something that is not understood."[6] In the novel the fur traders, or voyageurs, are afraid of catching and spreading the disease, so they leave Omakayas to die. However one of the traders, Hat, tells his wife, the brave and inimitable Old Tallow, about the girl, and she saves her and brings her back to Madeline Island.

The adoption of orphaned or abandoned children is a regular occurrence in Erdrich's fiction. The family trees that she includes at the beginning of many of her novels include adopted children in the family lines. For the Ojibwe adoption is a matter of hospitality, responsibility, and survival. The belief that all things are interconnected is an abiding one. As the tribe grows through the generations, small groups of neighboring clans intermarried; the tribe in a sense could thus be seen as a large, extended family with a strong communal identity. There are discernible kinship ties throughout the Ojibwe community, so to leave a child behind was to sacrifice a family member and diminish the tribe as a whole. Each member of the community had his or her role to play, and each life was precious. Omakayas's survival ensures the survival of the family, as she is naturally a healer; she provides a new lineage once she grows to adulthood and starts her own family, as is presented in *Chickadee.*

In *The Birchbark House,* Erdrich presents a portrait of a small band of Ojibwe and their everyday life. Instead of the one-dimensional portrait offered in frontier literature or popular culture, she presents a vivid, spacious depiction, giving the reader a full sense of the cultural, physical, and emotional life of the group. The book is organized around the seasons of the year, with nature providing the times at which certain rituals, traditions, and everyday chores are carried out. The birch tree and its bark, a central symbol throughout the book, mark the centrality of nature and the dependence of the tribe on the land. Birch bark is used to make everything from shelter to transportation. In the summer a birch-bark house is erected close to the lake to make access to fishing easier. Birch is used to make canoes to carry traders to different locations. The canoes could be used as means of carrying items in the water or on land and provided shelter to those who turned them upside down and crawled beneath. The bark was used to make markings or vessels for domestic use, the branches acted as utensils and tools, and the wood was used for fire. Like all items taken from nature, no part of the birch tree went to waste or was unused. Nature was respected. The land was sacred, to be cared for and protected, not stripped and tamed.

The notion of abusing the land, taking advantage of nature, was unthinkable, as it provided all that was necessary for survival: "As it grew dark, the family ate makuks of moose stew and fresh greens and berries, licked their fingers and bowls clean, and at last rolled themselves into warm, fluffy rabbit-skin blankets that still smelled of the cedary smoke of their winter cabin. They were glad to be close to fire, sleeping on soft grassy earth, under leafy sky, and best of all, near water. They fell asleep to the peaceful, curious, continual lapping sound of waves. The fresh wind across the big lake blew away the smoke of cooking fires and vanquished the mosquitoes that came out in whining droves and had plagued them in town" (12). Theirs was an elemental existence, and Omakayas and her family are constantly aware of the power of nature and the struggle to survive the elements. Fire, air, water, earth, wind are as life threatening as they are life sustaining: constant preparation is required to survive each of the seasons, and there are attendant rewards and inevitable dangers.

Daily and seasonal chores were essential for survival to the Ojibwe. The children of this time period had important responsibilities in addition to the sorts of daily chores contemporary children are accustomed to in the United States. Ojibwe children helped gather food and supplies, make clothing and shelter, hunt and cook, and clean and fortify the home. Each member of the family had a job to do. Survival was a collective effort; no one person bore sole responsibility for the group. For example Omakayas is a master tanner of moose hides, although much to her dismay. It is a messy business, which involves using a sharpened deer bone to scrape the insides from the moose hide and then tanning the hide with the brain of the animal. Her grandmother Nokomis teaches her that "each animal . . . has just enough brains to tan its own hide" (14). The words have a double-edged meaning, both practical and humorous; Omakayas finds nothing funny about the smelly mess, however, and dreads being asked to help her mother do the hard work. Nonetheless she "knew how important it was to tan the skin, how her mother would cut up the soft smoked hide and sew on the winter's makazins all summer," so she "finished her stew, cleaned the bowl out with sand at the shore of the lake, and waited with a sigh for her mother to ask her to fetch the deer-bone scraper" (17). In this description is a glimpse at the fullness of Erdrich's characters. She creates three-dimensional characters with a range of human emotions: sorrow, greed, happiness, regret, insincerity, and humor. There are no stock characters. Each family member has his or her own faults, strengths, idiosyncrasies, talents, and weaknesses. Omakayas's older sister, Angeline, can be "vain, cold-hearted sometimes" (10), and her younger brother, Pinch, is always hungry and greedy (11). When her father, Deydey, also called Mikwam ("Ice"), returns from his travels, "things were more exciting, things were more difficult, things were less predictable but somehow more secure" (52). The idyllic superficial portrayals of the noble savage or the depictions of primitive Native American characters encountered in much popular fiction are nowhere to be found. These are real flesh-and-blood people.

Erdrich also highlights the communal nature of the family and the shared responsibility each member has to ensure their survival. Unflagging reverence and attention is paid to both male and female tribal elders, who have position and power in the family and community. The elders pass down many of the traditions and rituals through storytelling and song. Working side by side, young and old contribute to all aspects of family life. Deydey is in the fur trade, building canoes for the trading companies and doing some trapping. Nokomis spends time gathering seeds and various plants for medicinal use. Old Tallow hunts, while Angeline and Yellow Kettle, Omakayas's mother, tend to domestic responsibilities. Pinch generally focuses his energies on mischief and annoying Omakayas between chores. Together each must face challenges in order to survive. For example much of the summer is spent making preparations for the harsh winter. Omakayas must keep crows from eating the corn the family has grown and harvested for winter use. The inextricable ties between man, nature, and the land, while life sustaining, can be a chore to manage. Omakayas values the respectful coexistence with nature learned from Nokomis, referring to various animal members of the community by name: "Grandfather Owl" (13), "One Horn" (183), "Andeg" (73). When she has caught the crows in a net, she remembers her grandmother's apology when trapping any living thing: "Forgive us, forgive us, we have need, we have need" (58). Omakayas learns not take an excess amount, only what is necessary. Instead of discarding the dead crows, the family honors them by making a meal of them.

Among the many depictions of everyday life Erdrich offers in the book, one major, life-altering event in the plot signals the onslaught of colonialism: the news of the white man from a family friend, Fishtail. *Chimookoman,* meaning "big knife," is the Ojibwe term that was used "to describe the non-Indian, or white people, who were travelling in larger numbers than ever to Ojibwa land and setting down their cabins, forts, barns, gardens, pastures, fences, fur-trading posts, churches, and mission schools" (76). The small town of La Pointe, abutting the Ojibwe territory, was becoming "more chimookoman every day," and there was talk of "sending the Anishinabeg to the west" (77). "They say we must leave the island," reports Fishtail (77). Albert LaPautre, a mixed-blooded French-Ojibwe married to Omakayas's aunt, thinks about taking his family west to where "government payments were made" (78). While he acknowledges that moving west had "hazards on the way—Dakota war parties, hunger, the threat of winter's dire weather"—Fishtail reasons that the Ojibwe "have to stop somewhere, someday. . . . West is where the spirits of the dead walk. If the whites keep chasing us west, we'll end up in the land of the spirits" —dead, in other words—which will "please them" (79). Deydey marvels at the chimookoman's voracious appetite for land: "They are like greedy children. Nothing will ever please them for long" (79). Fishtail agrees in a moment of prescience: "Not until they have it all. . . . All of our lands. Our wild-rice beds, hunting grounds, fishing streams, gardens. Not even when we are gone and they have the bones of our loved ones will they be pleased. . . . Before they were born, before they came into this world, the chimookoman must have starved as ghosts. They are infinitely hungry" (80).

Tensions are high in Omakayas's community, as everyone senses the beginning of something and the end of something else—their way of life. Battling nerves, disease, and possible dispossession in addition to tending to everyday matters of survival, Omakayas and her family are introduced to a threat, the U.S. government, that they never anticipated. Erdrich continues the story of Omakayas in *The Game of Silence,* as the threat grows and finally becomes the reason she loses her beloved home.

The Game of Silence

The Game of Silence, set in 1850, is a story of the dispossession of Ojibwe territory, the most traumatic consequence of colonization. Omakayas and her Ojibwe family, along with their friends and fellow clan members, face removal from their homeland.[7] This land is the place where generations of family members were born, lived and died, and are buried. Leaving everything they know and love for the unknown is a cataclysmic event for the community. This is the turning point in the series, when the inhabitants of Madeline Island are introduced to the consequences of Euro-American settlement. The fear, shame, insecurity, confusion, anger, and sorrow associated with this event are clearly described in *The Game of Silence,* which provides a rich portrait of the many costs of colonialism to the Ojibwe.

The first sign of trouble arrives with the appearance of "the raggedy ones" on the shores of Madeline Island. In the prologue, when Omakayas, looking out into the water of the lake, sees their approaching canoes, she realizes that "it was a day she would think of long after as one in which her fate, and that of her family, took a great looping turn."[8] She notices that the children are naked and the travelers are a "bony, hungry, anxious group" who "looked at the ground, fearfully and in shame" (1). Their chief, Miskobines or Red Thunder, implores Omakayas's family to open their hearts to his group, but "he hardly needed to urge kindness" (3): Miskobines is Fishtail's uncle, so kinship is immediately recognized and acknowledged. The family embraces the lowly travelers, "draping bare shoulders, and the pitiful naked children were covered, too, with all of the extra clothing that the people could find. Food was thrust into the hungry people's hands—strips of dried fish and bannock bread, maple sugar and fresh boiled meat. . . . One by one, family by family, the poor ones were taken to people's homes" (3). There is much anger and astonishment among Omakayas's family members at the state of these starving Ojibwe. The son of the leader, referred to as the Angry One, was "clearly struggling to look dignified" as he "mustered strength to stagger on ahead" (4). Omakayas observes that "the boy was proud and it had hurt him to have his ravenous eating observed" (6). Though they have been stripped of their homeland, the raggedy ones' dignity has been tested but not destroyed. However, having to accept handouts brings shame to many of the tribesmen. Self-sufficiency is crucial to survival, and the idea of being reliant on the kindness of another community is a test in humility for the Angry One and his people. Though it is an opportunity for Omakayas's family to help those in need, it is also a grim harbinger of times to come. How such a great and noble chief and his people could be brought to ruin is an ominous sign of the Ojibwe's vulnerability in the face of encroaching settlement.

Omakayas cannot believe the state in which she finds the young children, noting that even her "dolls had better clothing and better care" (5). A woman traveling with three children explains that the smallest is not hers: "We have been running for our lives. The Bwaanag wiped out our village. We left our gardens, our food caches, all of our kettles and our makazinan sitting by the doors. Some people even got left behind in the crazy mess. They were captured. That is why we have nothing. I don't know what happened to this baby's mother and father" (7). The orphaned child is adopted by Omakayas's family, in the same way and with the same feeling of kinship that marked her own adoption in *The Birchbark House*. The baby is called Bizhins (lynx) since he is always keenly looking at his surroundings, as if the attack on his village impressed upon him even at this young age the importance of constant vigilance. Many children lost their families to illness and tribal conflicts as pressure from the European traders and American settlers, in the form of disease and land grabbing, became more intense. Often the Ojibwe were forced out of their homes by neighboring Bwaanag, or Dakota Sioux, who were facing the loss of their own land and had nowhere else to go: "'There was a time when we had no quarrel with the Bwaanag,' said Deydey. 'They lived in their part of the world and we in ours. We even traded with them. But as the chimookomanag push us, so we push the Bwaanag. We are caught between two packs of wolves'" (21).

The eponymous game of silence is a task put to the children so that the adults can talk in peace without interruption. In past games there would be antics among the children to make one another laugh or scream. The game played on the evening after the raggedy ones come takes on greater importance than ever before; "nobody lost the game of silence," because all of the children stayed quiet, listening: "They would all fear to lose something huge, something so important that they never even knew that they had it in the first place. Who questions the earth, the ground beneath your feet? They had always accepted it—always here, always solid. That something was home" (19). The dawning realization that they may have to abandon the land that they love renders the children mute.

During the game the adults speak about the treaties in place with the U.S. government that they understood protected their homeland. The treaties were in a medium that the Ojibwe did not use in making promises or agreements: the written word. Omakayas is familiar with the language of the U.S. government: "The chimookomanag were the white people. The black marks that Mikwam spoke of were the writing that Angeline learned by day at the mission school in the town of La Pointe. The writing was very strange to Omakayas. Black marks that captured sounds. Tracks across paper or slate boards or birchbark that stood for words spoken. How did the odd scratching connect to the sounds? All a mysterious business, and one that her father, anyway, did not trust" (20). Erdrich juxtaposes the way the white man conducted transactions and contracts with the traditional ways of the Ojibwe, who made agreements through discussion and mutual understanding. The Ojibwe had a rich oral tradition, committing to memory any agreements through stories and songs: "The Ojibwe relied on memory. They repeated stories, songs, the words to promises and treaties. Everyone memorized all that was important. Although people scratched elaborate signs on birchbark and rolled them into scrolls, they relied on memory to go with the marks. Memory was Ojibwe writing. Things were not forgotten that way. Something about the black marks had gone wrong, Omakayas knew that. The black marks promised one thing, but the chimookomanag wanted to break that promise" (20). There is confusion surrounding the treaty. The gathered adults discuss the possibility that perhaps the U.S. government misunderstood or misremembered the terms of the treaty. Why else would they be trying to take the land from under Omakayas and her family? Ceding land did not have the same cultural meaning to the Ojibwe as it did to the U.S. government. The understanding of owning the land was very different for both groups. The idea of ownership of land was unthinkable and even ridiculous to the Ojibwe. Accordingly the idea of selling it was literally a foreign concept: "We signed a paper that said they could take the trees. We signed a paper that said they could take the copper from the earth, said the old chief Bizhiki, disturbed, 'we didn't say they could take the earth. . . . Who can take the earth?'" (20). Fishtail, who deals with traders and settlers, explains that the understanding of the relationship between humans and earth is very different for the chimookomanag: "When the chimookomanag open up the earth they believe they own it just like a kettle, just like this deerskin, just like this knife!" (21). Fishtail is one of the men who volunteer to be runners, scouts sent out to assess the situation. He goes on to explain the impending threat from the U.S. government: "Here is what had happened. The ogimaa or president of all of the chimookomanag had sent a message to the leaders of the Ojibwe. That message was simple. They must leave their homes. The ogimaa said that the government now owned the ground they lived on. It was needed for white settlers. He had issued a removal order. He had decided that land payments would be given out in a new place in the west. . . . But the western land was the home of the Bwaanag. The raggedy ones had tried to live there and look what had happened" (21).

Fishtail is alluding to the infamous Sandy Lake tragedy of 1850. In a scheme to trap the Ojibwe west of the Mississippi, making their removal west easier on the U.S. government, officials forced the Ojibwe to collect their 1850 annuity payment at Sandy Lake, Minnesota; three thousand people made the five-hundred-mile, late-autumn trip only to find no payments and no provisions at Sandy Lake. Four hundred men, women, and children—12 percent of the tribe—died.[9] Erdrich alludes to an actual event so that the reader can imagine in flesh-and-blood terms tragic incidents in the lives of the Ojibwe in the mid-nineteenth century. Thus the interrelated stories of her characters are woven into the Ojibwe's historical fight for survival.

In their struggle to understand and their confusion and panic, some tribal elders suggest that one of their own must have done something. They are confounded by the greed and treachery of the U.S. government and cannot grasp the possibility that it is unprovoked. One of the elders speculates that perhaps they "have done something to offend. One or two of our hot hearted brothers must have killed a chimookoman!" (22). Old Tallow agrees: "Perhaps we have broken our promise to be peaceful and treat them kindly! Send runners out. Send out michitweg. Find what our foolish brothers have done. Then we can punish the wrongdoers and stay here. *Right here*" (23). The adults are clearly frightened and scramble to find meaning in what is happening or identify the cause of the disenfranchisement.

The panic-stricken adults can offer little comfort to the children. Colonization created an abiding sense of insecurity in Ojibwe children and arguably in all displaced Native Americans. Omakayas reels with "the sudden thought that they could be removed from their home" as though it was a "crash of impossibility" (29). She implores her grandmother for reassurance: "They can't send us away, can they? . . . They can't do anything, really, Nokomis, can they? There are so few chimookomanag and so many of us!" (29). Nokomis replies, "The chimookomanag we see here are only the first drops of rain. A storm of them lives past the sunrise, in the east. They can flood us like a river. . . . We have seen what happens to others when they resist, go to war. The river wipes them out. Our way is different. We have always found out how to live with them, work with them, trade with them, even to marry them" (29–30). This group of Ojibwe fought along with the French traders against the British in the French and Indian War and learned to live peacefully among them. Perhaps this intermingling was a strategy of conquest on the part of the settlers, but the camaraderie persisted for more than two centuries. Deydey was a product of this relationship: "Deydey's grandfather had been a French trader, one of the first. Deydey had grown up in a house made of trees, like the cabin he'd built for his family. This alone marked him out as different" (30).

Even the American settlers in the neighboring town of La Pointe were living in harmonious coexistence with the Ojibwe. Though Omakayas's firsthand impression of the chimookomanag was the illness they brought to her island that decimated her biological family, her encounter with a young American settler in town, Clarissa is positive (44–46). Omakayas learns some of Clarissa's behaviors and traditions and is impressed by her kindness and generosity. Much of what she sees of the ways of Clarissa's people shocks and saddens her, however. The girl's clothes and shoes are highly impractical for the environment. Her people keep "slave animals" (48), fenced in and bound. But when Omakayas and her family must leave, she gives her beloved puppy to Clarissa, as she trusts her implicitly to take care of it despite the hostilities between the Ojibwe and Clarissa's people, the chimookomanag.

Religion and conversion practices are also introduced in the book, embodied by the Catholic priest in La Pointe, Father Baraga, who is referred to synecdochically as "Black Gown" because of his religious vestments (134). Old Tallow calls him "the stealer of souls" (186). An actual historical figure, Father Frederic Baraga was famous for transcribing the Ojibwe language into written form.[10] Erdrich presents him here with the same mission, in addition to his church-sanctioned one—conversion. He tells Omakayas that he is writing down their language: "He showed them the tracks. These written tracks formed a design that held the sounds of words—not just chimookoman but Ojibwe words. It was a marvel . . . that the signs his pen scratched out could be transformed into the things they said with their mouth" (188). Omakayas and Deydey are interested in learning, but Father Baraga offers to teach them only if they agree to be baptized, as, he cautions, that is "the only way to gain everlasting life" (188). In a moment of Erdrich's signature humor, Deydey inquires about his unbaptized ancestors and learns that they will not be in that afterlife. Deydey responds, "I want to see them!" (189). Why would he want to spend eternity without his loved ones? Father Baraga is frustrated in all of his attempts at converting Omakayas and her family and pities them. They, however, "pitied him right back" (188–89). Father Baraga also tries to teach the Ojibwe American ways of living. The concepts of land ownership and property are mingled with his teachings on Catholicism. In Western culture, he explains, “nobody moved from place to place, but stayed in one house all their lives” (187). The irony here is that the plight of the Ojibwe was caused precisely because the Euro-American settlers did not stay put permanently in Europe but decided to settle on Native American land.

Ultimately the family is forced to move; there has been no misunderstanding, only a breach of contract, and the U.S. government seizes the land for settlement. The emotional and spiritual impact of having to abandon a home and way of life is further developed in *The Porcupine Year,* the next book in the series, which is an account of Omakayas and her family’s travels to find a new homeland.

The Porcupine Year

The Porcupine Year follows Omakayas and family through the year 1852, during their harrowing journey from Madeline Island on Lake Superior to a new homeland in the Lake of the Woods or Lac du Bois area of Minnesota and Ontario, and all of the attendant dangers in that voyage. In this book Erdrich presents the emotional, physical, and psychological traumas of colonization, particularly those faced by the children. Erdrich writes, “Like so many Ojibwe and other Native Americans, Omakayas’s family were sent from their home by the United States government, to make way for European settlers.”[11] Essentially the Ojibwe were refugees in their own land. The perils of finding a new place to call home include desperately hunting for food, surviving the elements, and contending with hostile tribes. Omakayas’s family faces the possibility of extinction. It is only through their will to survive, some luck, and the collective effort of all members of the family that they survive and arrive at the home of kinfolk who have settled in Lake of the Woods.

One of the lasting effects of colonization was the progeny resulting from intermarriage or cross-cultural relationships and sexual liaisons among European traders and Native American women. *Métis,* meaning “mixed blood,” is the term used to describe these children. Though these couplings were commonplace, they did not offer much security for the mothers or children of the union. In her adult works, Erdrich connects this practice of intermarriage with the dilution of Native American blood, the cost of assimilation, and the loss of land rights by family inheritance. Often, however, the traders were only temporarily traveling in the New World and had families back at home in Europe, so many Métis children were raised solely by their mothers and maternal relatives, as was the case with Omakayas’s father, Deydey.

Deydey’s father was a French fur trader. Erdrich reveals the resulting identity crisis he suffered as a child. When his son Quill asks Deydey, “Did you ever know your father?” and Deydey replies that he met him once and “never cared to meet him again" (67). His father is the reason he favors his mother's side of the family and learned not to trust white people. As a child Deydey longed to meet his father, and in preparation for the highly anticipated occasion, his mother, Nokomis, teaches him how to speak a little French and "behave like a white person": "how to bow, how to shake hands, how to look at people's eyes, how to show his teeth in a bold, strange smile . . . and how to play chess" (68). The most poignant preparation is the memorization of the French phrase "Vous êtes mon père" (You are my father). Nokomis explained that his father was a "rich and important man," and when Deydey was ten years old, together they walked one hundred miles to the fort where he was staying. Upon entering the establishment where the trader and his friends were finishing dinner, Deydey delivered his well-rehearsed line to his father and was met with jeering, hysterical laughter, as his father and companions "wept at the absurdity of it" (69). In that moment Deydey's Ojibwe identity was established, and his French heritage was only a cruel reminder of that day.

Erdrich also highlights the power of storytelling to soothe the confused and frightened children. The timeline of each book in the Birchbark House series follows the seasons, and in the winter sections of the books characters tell traditional stories: "The Ojibwe told stories only in the winter" (34). Timing is important for the old stories; they are told "when the frogs and snakes are sleeping" (37), because "if underground and underwater creatures heard the stories, they might repeat them to the powerful underwater spirits, or the great spirits of the animals, who might be angry at the Ojibwe for talking about them" (38). More important are the many psychological, emotional, and spiritual benefits of the tales: "Nokomis told stories to keep up their spirits. She told stories to teach them, to heal them," and as "the little family mourned and recovered, she told stories to help them gain their strength and laugh again" (122). Storytelling is valued as a survival technique as much as entertainment. By distracting the little ones with traditional stories, tribal elders are able to assuage fears while teaching lessons and sharing Ojibwe traditions.

In addition to stories of old, the family hears disturbing rumors during their journey through Sandy Lake. The U.S. government's plan for the Ojibwe involves "making one big home for all of us, over near the land of the Bwaan [Dakota Sioux]" (45). Deydey has his doubts about the plan: "He did not trust the white people, the chimookomanag. He did not trust the chiefs. He did not trust the one they called 'great father' off in Washington. 'He is not my great father,' Deydey would say. 'I have seen him starve our people. I have seen him take our land. No father kills his children and leaves them homeless!' So Deydey did not trust the idea of one big homeland for all of the Anishinaabeg" (45). The proposal for all of the midwestern Native American communities to share a relatively small tract of land is untenable. "No home would be big enough. We do things very differently, even though we speak the same language," Deydey explains (46). There could be fighting and not enough food for the large numbers of Ojibwe. An additional concern is encroaching on established Bwaanag land, which could prove deadly. For centuries the Ojibwe had engaged in war with the Bwaanag, so relations between the two tribes were strained. While they respected the Bwaanag and traded with them, the Ojibwe "sent war parties into Bwaan country and came back with deaths to boast of, with horses, or with captives to replace any Anishinabeg victims who had been lost to a war party" (75). The idea of sharing land and living among the Bwaanag was ludicrous, though at this point, as Deydey points out, "the chimookomanag didn't care whose hunting land they stepped on, Bwaanag or Anishinabeg—they stole it just the same" (76). Perhaps "the real enemy they all faced was the growing threat of white settlers" (76). In many of Erdrich's novels, particularly the children's books, warring tribes often disrupt idyllic tribal life, so that a picture of the complex social relations among tribes is offered rather than a facile, one-dimensional portrait of Native American life. The boundaries and rules by which different tribes interacted, though they spoke different languages and had different values and traditions, were always understood to be law, collectively agreed upon, sometimes sacred, and usually binding. Disputes were settled through war or negotiation, but the concept of ownership was not an issue. There was no frame of reference to guide ownership practices. Different tribes had a sense of the boundaries and, more often than not, respected them. In the face of impending encroachment, however, the differences in tribal identity were of no consequence. The U.S. officials did not make distinctions but instead lumped all of the Native American peoples into one group of primitives who were occupying land that they desired for settlement.

Once the family settles at Lake in the Woods, Omakayas still struggles with the insecurity born out of their displacement. She asks Nokomis, "And we will live here. . . . won't we? For a long time to come?" (181). The questions about place and home are a central, nagging problem in establishing emotional and mental security. Omakayas has been uprooted from the place she calls her homeland twice at this point in the series, and the moving is not finished. Omakayas is not yet home, as readers of the next book in the series, *Chickadee,* discover.

Chickadee

Chickadee is set in 1866, after the American Civil War and during the ongoing western expansion and settlement of Native American land. While slavery had been abolished with the Emancipation Proclamation, the Native American "problem" persisted for the U.S. government, and U.S.-Native relations deteriorated rather than improved under Abraham Lincoln and subsequent U.S. presidents.[12] The primary action of the story is the search for the eponymous character Chickadee, son of Omakayas, who has been kidnapped and taken to the plains, far away from the Lake of the Woods and the prairie; to the booming town of Saint Paul; and ultimately to the small settlement in Pembina. Chickadee's disappearance precipitates a move for the whole extended family, which is analogous to the forced removal of Ojibwe during that time. The boy's kidnapping is a plot device that sets up the opportunity for Erdrich to explore the traumatic dispossession of land facing the Ojibwe.

As recounted in *The Birchbark House, The Game of Silence,* and *The Porcupine Year,* the Ojibwe were a people on the move in the mid-nineteenth century, forced from their homeland by various federal government initiatives. While *The Game of Silence* and *The Porcupine Year* illustrate the difficulties of migration into Dakota Sioux territory, *Chickadee* finds the family confronted with the Métis and American settlers on the plains. Here Erdrich creates a picture of the harsh new landscape for the family, who are unaccustomed to the dry, flat plains. On Spirit Island and Madeline Island, Omakayas and her family's dependence on the land and evident understanding of its attendant flora and fauna are clearly depicted. In this new land, the family must adapt to new ways of living, eating, interacting, and surviving. Assimilation in the service of survival confronts Omakayas's family in a profound way in their search for Chickadee. They must interact with Métis, Dakota Sioux, Euro-American settlers, and Catholic clergy as Chickadee and his family navigate their way back to each other.

In *Chickadee* the reader gets an impression of the pressures of religion and racism faced by the Anishinaabe at this time of turmoil in Native American history. Presented with the challenges of survival and of negotiating with settlers and neighboring tribes, the Ojibwe were forced to create a new life, in a new landscape, in close proximity to others outside the tribe with different traditions, languages, social mores, and religious practices. Chickadee, in his escape from the brutish Métis brothers Babiche and Batiste, encounters a priest, a "black robe," traveling with a group of nuns and a mother superior; hearing them refer to each other as "father" and "sister" and "mother," he mistakes the religious group for a "happy family."[13] His assumption illustrates his unfamiliarity with the Catholic clergy and the extent to which the idea of family is ingrained. While he is shown kindness by the group, the mother superior refers to Chickadee on more than one occasion as a "filthy savage" (87) and as "typically pagan" (89); with a rough scouring brush and lye soap, she attempts to "wipe the dirt of the ancients" off him (93). Armed with religious values that cast Native Americans as the uncleansed, Euro-American settlers viewed their conquest partly as God's work, ensuring salvation for the pagans. The colonial attitude toward the indigenous people of the land the settlers occupied is a reflection of the Western values that rationalized their supremacist stance over Native Americans.

Even when Chickadee meets up with his uncle Quill, Omakayas's brother, on his way to Saint Paul for trade in an oxcart convoy of traders, he witnesses the racism rampant in all transactions with European Americans. When Quill takes out a notebook to write down prices for his goods, a trader exclaims, "Looka here, this savage is writin'" (152). Though assimilation through language was encouraged by the U.S. government in order to make business relationships easier, the customary interactions with the Euro-American traders often became moments of humiliation. The Ojibwe resignedly understood this to be an unavoidable part of the negotiations of commerce. This is why Deydey wants all of his children and grandchildren to learn English and be schooled in the chimookoman ways, in order to understand contracts, agreements, and even insults exchanged between them and the white man. English is the privileged language of commerce and of colonization, so learning the language helps alleviate one of the many disadvantages of dealing with the colonists.

Chickadee's upbringing has been fairly sheltered, so he is unfamiliar until this point with the dominant culture. The honor among strangers, recognition of kinship, respect for nature, and sense of community on the oxcart convoy was more in line with his own understanding of the world, so the bustling, impersonal commerce of Saint Paul is unsettling. In fact it shakes Chickadee to the core to have his worldview altered so dramatically and the natural world so irrevocably. Saint Paul is the first place in which Chickadee encounters the true impact of the settlement of Native lands. Seeing mansions on hilltops, he is awed by the sheer scope of the devastation of the natural world: "Chickadee could see that they had cut down every tree in sight. He could feel that they were pumping up the river and even using up the animals. He thought of the many animals whose dead hides were bound and sold in St. Paul in one day. Everything that the Anishinabeg counted on in life, and loved, was going into this hungry city mouth. The mouth, this city, was wide and insatiable. It would never be satisfied, thought Chickadee dizzily, until everything was gone" (155).

As the search for Chickadee takes them to the town of Pembina, Omakayas's family finds that Quill and his wife, Margaret, have settled into a small, quiet cabin. Margaret wants the family to settle in this new territory, but she does not want them encroaching on the home she has built with Quill. She is a Catholic Métis and accustomed to different ways of everyday living. When Deydey, her father-in-law, explains that the family would like to wait for Quill's return, Margaret hesitates and looks "worriedly at her bed," clearly not wanting to share her living space; she suggests they try acquiring one of the abandoned cabins in town. This signals more changes, including the breakdown of the extended family, as they venture farther away from their old life on the island. The joint family domestic dwelling that characterized earlier days in Omakayas's community is now a perceived nuisance, which is a seismic shift in the paradigm of clan living. The making of the compact nuclear family, comprising husband, wife, and children until they are grown and set out to start their own lives, begins. In another sense the individual family unit trumps the communal family. The assumption of stretching out—that there is land for everyone—rather than just using what is necessary also marks a dramatic shift in the sensibilities of the Native American. Margaret, while wanting her husband's family to stay in town and even settle there permanently, does not want them "to take over her carefully groomed cabin" (102). Utilitarian practices in the interest of conservationism were formerly privileged over luxury living or excess. By taking only what was needed from the land, the Ojibwe guarded against squandering life-sustaining resources in order to ensure survival.

A prime example of this conservative way of life is the family cabin. Though it is cramped, the family sets it up with small spaces for all: "The little cabin was propped up and stabilized now, and the logs were tightly chinked with mud. The floor was tamped down and then covered with rush mats. Everyone took off their moccasins when entering, so the mats stayed nice and clean. Fishtail had traded for a small square stove, and the wood was neatly stacked beside. He and Angeline had roped off a small room in one corner. In another corner, Mikwam and Yellow Kettle slept. Omakayas and Animikiins had their part of the room too. Nokomis curled near the stove with Zozie and Makoons. And Two Strike slept outside with the horses" (164–65).

Each member of the family participates in the upkeep of the homestead and the family's survival, including by gathering resources. Nokomis tends to her seeds; Angeline take care of household chores; the children tend to the fence and the grounds; Fishtail acquire through trade; and Deydey learns to build a cart so the family can participate in buffalo hunting the Métis way (165). There is still an abundance of buffalo in this volume of the Birchbark House series, but that will ultimately change. Deydey must learn to build carts since he can no longer make canoes from plentiful birch trees. The new landscape forces the family to adapt or perish.

Recollecting the birches of their original homeland, the family notices the absence of the tree during their travels. Though they had carried some birch bark with them for shelter, it blows away during the first snowstorm they experience in this new landscape, the plains. Its loss brings to the family the realization that "they were now people of the Great Plains" and that such houses were for people of the woods (64). Not only the birches but also trees of every type are disappearing. Chickadee's first impression of Saint Paul is of a city of dead trees, as the chimookomanag are stripping the land of them for the construction of buildings. While the Ojibwe could make much of what they needed out of birch bark, the settlers use wood to build ornate mansions in the cities.

Trees are one of the most important symbols in Erdrich's work. They are of the land, Mother Earth. Nature has a language, and trees are one of that language's underlying structures—an essential part of the syntax. Their ominous vanishing becomes symbolic of the existential threat faced by the family, and the Ojibwe as a people, in the times to come. Erdrich will surely continue in upcoming installments of the Birchbark House series to recount Omakayas's family's trials and tribulations on their historical journey of survival and their desperate search for a place to call home.

CHAPTER 6

Poetry and Nonfiction

Though many of Erdrich's early readers viewed her as both a poet and a novelist, Erdrich admits that "I stopped thinking like a poet back when I started writing narrative poems. Occasionally I get some poetry, and I'll write poetry for as long as I can. But it is as though I've been temporarily excused by the novel, and it wants me back. So I usually put whatever poetry I would have written into the novel. I only keep a few of my poems as poems."[1] Erdrich's poetic impulses are evident in the lyrical style of her fiction, with its poetic description, symbolism, imagery, metaphors, and songs. Though she creates poetic passages in each novel that could arguably stand alone as individual prose poems, Erdrich's primary focus has been on the novel form throughout her career.

Poetry

Erdrich has published three volumes of poetry: *Jacklight* (1984), which includes the much-anthologized "Dear John Wayne" and "Indian Boarding School: The Runaways"; *Baptism of Desire* (1989), a more intimate and spiritual collection that explores her Ojibwe heritage, Catholic identity and motherhood and continues a series of prose poems begun in *Jacklight* titled "The Potchikoo Stories"; and *Original Fire: Selected and New Poems* (2003). This last volume includes a number of poems from the previous two books along with nineteen new poems. A look at selected poems from each of the three volumes gives readers a glimpse of Erdrich's continuing commitment to celebrate Ojibwe forms of storytelling and myth, to reveal the environmental consequences of colonization on the natural world, and to relate the cultural confusion and identity struggles of the colonized subject—a consequence of the assimilation policies of Euro-American institutions in the New World.

Jacklight, published in the same year as *Love Medicine,* includes forty-four poems and is divided into five parts: "Jacklight," "Runaways," "Hunters," "The Butcher's Wife." and "Myths." Each part contains poems that are thematically linked, giving readers a sense of the many aspects of Erdrich's cultural identity. The subject matter varies from Ojibwe spirituality and cultural colonialism to the German immigrant experience and from the everyday to the mythic. The first section contains only one poem, the titular "Jacklight." The poem introduces themes that occupy the rest of the collection and, really, the rest of Erdrich's oeuvre. The themes of nature, love, sex, power (and more specifically subjugation), revenge, perseverance, and survival are central to Erdrich's fictional worlds and are clearly voiced in this volume. The literary space of the poem offers a distilled version of these themes that are addressed in long form in her novels, and Erdrich's readers will easily find similarities between the concerns she raises in the poem and those of her novels.

The action of the poem deals with the hunting practice of using a blinding light called a jacklight to paralyze and disorient prey. "Jacklighting" is considered an unsportsmanlike method of hunting wildlife. It signals weakness and insecurity in the hunter who resorts to such sly and deceptive means. Through the metaphor of jacklighting, Erdrich offers a picture of a male-female relationship and its attendant power struggles. Love and sexuality are seen as analogous to the hunter-prey relationship, but the hunting metaphor also relates to the various ways in which the Ojibwe were hunted or oppressed by Euro-American settlers yet persevered through patience and tact. Erdrich includes an epigraph from R. W. Dunning's *Social and Economic Change among the Ojibwa* (1959), which explains that the word for flirting is the same word used for hunting in Ojibwe and that the word "connotes both using force in intercourse and also killing a bear with one's bare hands" (3). From the beginning of the text, then, Erdrich introduces the themes of nature and mankind, sex and love, power and powerlessness, and hunter and hunted in both Ojibwe and English terms. These are the themes that take up the rest of the text. And as the poem progresses through a scene of hunters using nebulous means for hunting their prey, by the end the hunted have become the hunters:

> It is their turn now,
> Their turn to follow us. Listen,
> They put down their equipment.
> It is useless in the tall brush.
> And now they take the first steps, not knowing
> how deep the woods are and lightless
> How deep the woods are (4)

The prey draws the hunters deep into the woods, into nature, and away from a position of power. The hunters' equipment is useless in nature, where it is man against the environment. Entrance into the woods signals a shift into unfamiliar territory for the hunters. Without the tools of colonization, the colonizers are disoriented and powerless. The Ojibwe, like the prey in the poem, endured the predation of colonialism, forced removal, land allotment acts, and the reservation system. Through unshakeable resilience and a deep connection to the land, they persevered. The roots of the Ojibwe are as deeply established as the tall brush, and the hunter, the colonizer, is unaware of the power of this rootedness. In this way "Jacklight" sets the tone for the rest of the collection, in which various speakers, both real and mythical, relate the various tragedies and triumphs of existence, in the realm of everyday life and through folklore and mythology.

The titles of the remaining sections in the collection reflect the subject matter in each grouping. Notably the "Runaways" section contains "Dear John Wayne" and "Indian Boarding School: The Runaways." In keeping with the theme of colonialism and assimilation, "Indian Boarding School" finds Erdrich poeticizing the experience of young Ojibwe children taken away from their families and placed in residential boarding schools, often far from their reservations, in an effort to assimilate, Christianize, and generally Westernize them. Erdrich explained in an interview with Joseph Bruchac about the particular kind of running away described in the poem: "It's running home; it's not running away from home. The kids who are talking in this poem are children who've been removed from their homes, their cultures, by the Bureau of Indian Affairs or by any sort of residential school or church school. Many kinds of schools were set up to take Indian children away from their culture and parents and loved ones and re-acculturate them. So, it is about the hopelessness of a child in that kind of situation. There is no escape. The sheriff is always waiting at midrun to take you back."[2] The trauma of this government policy is a subject Erdrich also writes about in her fiction, illustrating one of the ways her poetry serves as an important counterpart to her fiction.

As early as 1984, Erdrich brought to the attention of Western readers the common practice of placing young Native American children in military-style boarding schools, a practice that still haunts many Ojibwe and other Native Americans. The boarding school system is widely ignored or given little attention in the annals of U.S. history but is part of the cultural fiber and historical trauma of twentieth-century indigenous peoples. The overall tone of the poem is one of searing isolation, but the opening line appears hopeful: "Home's the place we head for in our sleep" (11). The children are seemingly not colonized in the space of their dreams; they enjoy a subconscious freedom there. Only their bodies are subjected to systematic assimilation. This sense of comfort or escape is a pitiful irony, however, since the waking hours of these children is taken up with the suffering and shame of menial work, and the devastating effect on their psyches and self-esteem is clearly part of their lived reality. There is an intense sense of that place, home, but it is not within reach.

Reality for the students is the boarding school—the isolating and identity-stripping confines of the institution in which they live and work. As they are forced to do shameful things, even their clothing reflects the humiliation they feel: "All runaways wear dresses, long green ones, / the color you would think shame was. We scrub / the sidewalks down because it's shameful work" (11). The modest, austere, unadorned garments reflect no sign of the students' vibrant Native identity. The uniform strips the students of individuality, as well. Where the color green should symbolize youth, nature, and growth, instead it connotes shame, conformity, and stagnation. Green, in this context, is an institutional color, not natural, vibrant, or nurturing. Erdrich also uses words that reflect physical manifestations of the damage inflicted on the students throughout the poem: *scars, lacerations, cracks, hurts, worn-down welts, punishments, injuries* (11). Running from and returning to a place that is no place, the runaway students chart a course through life to home, led by experience; they learn that "riding scars / you can't get lost" (11). It is through these permanent reminders, the physical, emotional, and spiritual scars of their harrowing boarding school ordeal, that the children map their lives and remember who they are at the core—Native American. The irony here is that those very assimilation practices often have the opposite effect; the boarding school experience can be a prime motivator for the creation of a strong sense of self and Native American cultural awareness in the children subjected to this identity-erasing system.

The remaining sections in the collection include "Hunters," which deals with both human relationships and the natural world in poems such as "Captivity," the speaker of which is Mary Rowlandson, who is known for her dramatic captivity narrative. In this poem she struggles with her Puritan sensibilities and revulsion over Native American ways as well as her odd identification with, and simmering sexual attraction to, her Native American captor. "The Butcher's Wife" section focuses on Erdrich's German ancestry and contains the seeds of the novels *The Beet Queen* and *The Master Butchers Singing Club.* Lastly the "Myths" section introduces various characters from Ojibwe mythology in such poems as "Windigo" and "Old Man Potchikoo," the title character of which appears in a series of folkloric vignettes in *Baptism of Desire* and *Original Fire,* as well. The "Old Man Potchikoo" section is curious, as it is a series of prose poems recalling the narrative style of much of Erdrich's fiction rather than being in a poetic meter; the pieces thus stand out from the rest of the poetry in the collection. Arguably Erdrich's fiction is also prose poetry with its lyrical aspect, deep imagery, and rhythmic quality, but the Potchikoo stories feel distinctly prosaic in the poetic context in which they appear. The stories are also included in *The Oxford Book of Modern Fairy Tales* (1993). The trickster figure lends itself to poetic treatment, as much of ancient mythology is transcribed in verse or poetic prose. Alison Lurie, the editor of *The Oxford Book of Modern Fairy Tales,* describes the series as employing "the Native American trickster tale as a starting-point for a celebration of Dionysian energy."[3] Lurie searches for a Western correlative to describe Erdrich's work for the benefit of Western readers. The idea that these folktales are from an aboriginal culture, with its own mythology and formal structure, goes against the dominant impulse of Western literary analysis. Perhaps Erdrich creates a new genre, defying categories, in these stories. If so then the Potchikoo stories serve as a meaningful introduction to Erdrich's distinctive style and dedication to Ojibwe forms of storytelling rather than as a call for the reader to squeeze her genre-defying narratives into prescribed forms for easy consumption.

The Potchikoo stories represent the function of storytelling and myth in Ojibwe culture and in Erdrich's own writing. These trickster tales are only one aspect of *Baptism of Desire,* and a brief overview of the whole collection is in order before proceeding to a full discussion of Potchikoo. In this second collection of poetry, Erdrich's spiritual self is more evident than in *Jacklight.* Each part of the text is devoted in some way to her Catholic upbringing and her questioning of it. Erdrich does return to many of the same themes as in *Jacklight:* the mythic, the ordinary, and the mystic are all present in the poems of the text. The volume is divided into five parts: the first grapples with her Catholic heritage; the second returns to her German ancestry, with Mary Kroger and Rudy J. V. Jacklitch, characters introduced in *Jacklight*, making cameo appearances; the third part is taken up entirely by one poem, "Hydra," which describes a serpent-like female energy; the fourth part continues "The Potchikoo Stories," told in seven prose poems; and the fifth and final part opens Erdrich's domestic world to readers in a series of poems dealing with the personal, the domestic, and the everyday rituals of a woman's life. The varied roles of women, from mythological being to mother, from German immigrant to saint, take up much of the collection, whatever the overarching theme. In a note to the mythological poem "Hydra," Erdrich explains that most of the poems in the collection were written in the wee hours during her pregnancies: "'Hydra' and most of the other poems in this book were written between the hours of two and four in the morning, a period of insomnia brought on by pregnancy."[4] Cleary the broad range of meditations, from spiritual to domestic, seem to reflect a mother contemplating her own sense of identity as a woman, a spiritual being, and an ethnically diverse individual wielding a powerful, if not mythological, feminine creative force.

While each section of *Baptism of Desire* reveals pieces of Erdrich's Ojibwe identity, the fourth part, "Potchikoo's Life after Death," focuses exclusively on the character's negotiation through the afterlife in an amalgamated Catholic and Ojibwe spiritual landscape. With humor and pathos, Erdrich describes his travels to Catholic Heaven, then to Catholic Hell, where the forsaken spend eternity in suburban midwestern damnation chained to old Sears catalogs, and then to the Ojibwe afterlife, when an off-road detour leads him to a great, empty pasture where he finds others roasting game around a bonfire and laughing. Finally Potchikoo finds his way back to his beloved wife, Josette, when his sexual desires force him back into the living world. Josette, an Ojibwe Catholic, sends Potchikoo on his soulful travel to the afterlife with a loaf of fry bread. She "set some bread by the door for him to take on his journey to the next world" (51). The Ojibwe believe in leaving provisions for loved ones in preparation for travels to the afterlife. Though Josette is a believer who daily attends Mass, she cannot abandon certain traditional Ojibwe beliefs about the afterlife. In this way Erdrich cleverly fuses both Catholic and Ojibwe spiritual beliefs throughout the narrative. The Ojibwe afterlife is one of sensuality and gratification. Earthly pleasures such as food, laughter, and sex are to be found in abundance, so even a practicing Catholic Ojibwe would find it difficult to surrender this notion of heaven. In the rest of the story Erdrich pits both belief systems against one another, but she does so in a way that presents neither Catholicism nor Ojibwe spirituality as superior or more virtuous. The stories reflect a deep internal struggle of the colonized Ojibwe to reconcile disparate beliefs, to live among and with rather than precariously on the threshold.

When Potchikoo reaches the pearly gates, he finds Saint Peter waiting, "dressed in a long, brown robe, just as the nuns and priests had always said he would be" (52). Potchikoo identifies himself, at which point Peter produces a large book from beneath his robe to review a list of sins. Potchikoo is unnerved by the length of time Peter runs his finger down the length of the page, "but as it happened, there was only one word there. The word *Indian*," at which point Peter states, "You'll have to keep walking" (52). Erdrich is not subtle in her criticism of Catholic judgment. In a review of *Baptism of Desire*, Helen Jaskoski characterized Potchikoo's travels as "something of a Dantean journey through heaven and hell."[5] In Dante's Hell, however, the system by which sinners are placed in one of the various rings is a complex and detailed one, accounting for a long list of depravities. Erdrich's vision of the afterlife features a Catholic Heaven casting out Potchikoo for one grievous sin: being Ojibwe. Though he received an education from "nuns and priests," his status as an

Ojibwe is the one and only sin barring him from entering the Catholic paradise. Many Ojibwe came to believe through an often racist missionary education that despite welcoming and adopting Christianity, salvation was not ensured for the Native American. The identity-stripping assimilation practices left many feeling inadequate or insecure in their native skin, physically and spiritually. It is Erdrich's characters such as Potchikoo who successfully navigate their way through the forced integration of non-Ojibwe cultural values with humor, strength, self-confidence, and a playful irreverence that symbolizes their people's vitality and resilience. Thus Potchikoo anticipates some of Erdrich's most beloved characters, such as Nanapush and Mooshum.

Potchikoo's exploits are continued in *Original Fire* in a section titled "Saint Potchikoo," in which the title character spends his days carving a statue for Josette so that he will always be a presence in her life, even after his death. The townspeople speculate that "divine light had descended on a habitual miscreant" and that "the old rascal had converted and was carving the Virgin Mary, or maybe Saint Joseph."[6] After Mass on Easter morning, a group gathers around Potchikoo and Josette's cabin for the grand unveiling. Readers of Potchikoo's earlier escapades will likely anticipate the irreverent figure shrouded under a curtain: "Silence. There was a lot of silence from the people. Potchikoo interpreted their silence as awe, and for sure, he felt the awe of it too. For the statue of himself had all of his unmistakable features, including the fantasy of his favorite part of himself at its most commanding" (51–52). The juxtaposition between the reverence with which the townspeople, and Potchikoo himself, approach the event and the shocking revelation of the stark biology of the statue is characteristic of Erdrich in its trickster sensibility and resulting humor.

Original Fire picks up other threads from the previous poetry volumes as well. The nineteen new poems in the collection attest to Erdrich's ongoing treatment of the theme of colonization in her work. Particularly a pair of new poems, "Buffalo Prayer" and "Rez Litany," feature two different but nonetheless related aspects of the lasting effects of colonization: on the natural world in one and on the Ojibwe people in the other. Erdrich offers readers a condensed version of Native American history. In both poems she adopts the tone of Catholic prayers to indict the Church for its many sins against the Ojibwe and to recognize the irrevocable damage inflicted upon the land and its inhabitants in the service of advancing Euro-American civilization. From within the oppressor's own forms, Erdrich is able to highlight the injustices of the colonizers who employed religious means for monetary and political ends and to reveal the lasting effects of colonization on the environment.

"Buffalo Prayer" begins "Our Lady of the Buffalo Bones, pray for us. / Our Lady of the bales of skins and rotting hulks / from which our tongues alone were taken, / pray for us" (122). The speaker, ostensibly the buffalo of the title, bemoans the practice of European traders and American settlers of only taking the parts of the buffalo deemed sellable—the tongue, which was considered a delicacy, and sometimes the hide. In stark contrast the Ojibwe lived among the buffalo and came to rely on the animal as an integral part of survival. No part of the animal was discarded or wasted. The buffalo's hide, flesh, tallow, and bones provided food, tools, clothing, shelter, medicine, utensils, cookware, and ceremonial items. Symbolically the absence of a tongue means the buffalo have no voice with which to pray and must ask for intercession. Erdrich's poem, then, provides a voice with which the buffalo's prayer will be heard.

The speaker in the poem continues to list animals, along with the buffalo, who have no voice to explain that the killing of the buffalo also affects the interconnected nature of the ecosystem and that shifting populations or the introduction of other animals and crops affects the sensitive balance: "Our Lady of the Poisoned Meat / and of the wolves who ate / and whose tongues swelled until they burst / Our Lady of the Eagles Dropping from the Sky / Our Lady of the Sick Fox and of the Lurching Hawk" (122). Poisoning any member of the animal population can have dramatic consequences for the rest of the food web; predators and prey are connected in the natural world in a symbiotic relationship. If an animal is poisoned and its body is left abandoned, then any predator or scavenger looking for food will unwittingly face the same end as the poisoned animal. On a spiritual level, the killing of these animals has other consequences as well. For Ojibwe tribes animals play a central spiritual and social role. Each tribe is a clan, or dodem, named after a specific animal. That animal is a sacred being to the tribe and must be revered and protected. Erdrich's Ojibwe family is from both the Crane and the Bear clans. Animals represent the soul and identity of many Ojibwe clans.

The poem not only recalls the appalling devastation of the buffalo but also exposes the often-disregarded impact of colonization on the Great Plains and the Midwest. "Our Lady of the Box Cars of Skulls, / pray for us whose bones have nourished / the ordered cornfields that have replaced / the random grass / which fed and nurtured and gave us life" (122). The shift from a hunter-gatherer way of life to an agricultural one was devastating to many tribes, including the Ojibwe. Accustomed to hunting buffalo as needed, the Ojibwe had to relearn how to live in the ever-changing landscape. The explorers, settlers, and traders introduced cows, chickens, horses, new plants, and crops to the New World and ultimately claimed the best farming and grazing land as their own. As a consequence the land could not support the few buffalo that escaped extermination. The grazing grasses were coopted by cattle and horses or transformed into farmland, so the buffalo diminished to near extinction. They were no longer a welcome element or necessary part of the new landscape for the settlers, even though they were essential to the Ojibwe way of life. Killing the buffalo, as a consequence of settling the land, was one of many means of destroying the Ojibwe way of life and forcing upon the Ojibwe a new way of being in the world.

In terms of colonization's effect on the Ojibwe, Erdrich creates in "Rez Litany" a scathing satirical liturgy in which a number of imagined saints are petitioned for intercession in a variety of ways, to cure the unholy effects of the "Holy Colonial Church" (123) on Native Americans. Assimilation through attendance in boarding schools, a topic Erdrich takes up in several novels, is alluded to in the poem. The speaker intones the first petition to "Saint Assimilus, / patron of residential and government / boarding schools, whose skin was dark / but who miraculously bled white milk / for all to drink" (123). The dark and white imagery reminds readers of the attempted erasure of indigenous identity from the inside out, as skin color did not change no matter what degree of assimilation practices were imposed upon the schoolchildren. The milk, which should be nourishing, produces "gut aches" in the Native American children unused to Euro-American food and drink, particularly cow's milk, and unfamiliar with Euro-American values, which were force-fed to them. Changing eating habits, disorienting the children with unfamiliar food, was a highly effective way to create a dependence in the students in the boarding school system. Even the school diet had acculturation as an objective.

The speaker prays also to Good Saint Pyromane, "Enemy of the BIA / Deliver us from those who seek to bury us / in files and triplicate documents and directives" (124). The BIA, or Bureau of Indian Affairs, which operates under the auspices of the U.S. Department of the Interior, is the governmental agency in charge of all matters relating to Native American issues, including land management, health care, and education. Through the BIA Native American tribes were given rations, referred to as commodity food, in exchange for land rights, another consequence of colonization. The rations, consisting primarily of the pantry staples milk, flour, sugar, butter, and coffee, were often in short supply due to delayed or spoiled deliveries. The speaker alludes to the nutritional quality of the food in prayers to the "twin saints of commodity food / Saint Bloatinus and Saint Cholestrus / who were martyred at the stake of body fat / and who preside now in heaven / at the gates of the Grand Casino Buffet" (123).

Historically, aside from food, alcohol was another colonial negotiating tool used to win tribal land, resulting in countless Native Americans' suffering the effects of alcohol abuse and an alarming prevalence of alcoholism in contemporary tribal communities. The speaker prays to the "powerful triumvirate" of Saint Bingeous, Saint Odium, and Saint Tremens to "intercede for us / drunks stalled in the bars, float our asses off the cracked stools / and over to the tribal college" (124). Alcoholism, poor education, teen pregnancy, and poverty are the inheritance of Native American children born on reservations. The speaker ends with saints Primapara, Gravida, and Humpenenabackseat, patrons of "unsafe teenage sex / and fourteen-year-old mothers" to "pray for us now and at the hour of our birth, / amen" (125). Erdrich cleverly and poignantly changes the last line of the Hail Mary prayer, which asks Mary to pray for Catholic petitioners "now and at the hour of our death." For the Ojibwe in Erdrich's poem, death would be a release; the desperate prayers are needed to get through life. Erdrich's poem enumerates the ways colonialism enacted the breakdown of the traditional Native American community and left a legacy of tribulation. The numerous social issues afflicting Native Americans—the loss of territory, the irrevocable destruction of the natural landscape, and the daily reminders of colonialism—are the utmost concerns in Erdrich's poetry.

Nonfiction Works

Louise Erdrich's introduction to a 1993 edition of John Tanner's *The Falcon,* a classic nineteenth-century account of a Kentucky man's life among the Ojibwe, offers insights regarding her own autobiographical writing. She writes that "the Tanner narrative possesses the vigor and disorganization of an authentic life."[7] Those words could easily apply to Erdrich's own similarly vigorous and seemingly "disorganized" creative nonfiction: the memoir of motherhood *The Blue Jay's Dance: A Birth Year* (1995) and the travel memoir *Books and Islands in Ojibwe Country: Traveling in the Land of My Ancestors* (2003). Both texts are characterized by the singular narrative strategies found in her fiction; indeed both read like an Erdrich novel. Erdrich uses the Ojibwe language, historical facts, character studies, humor, and pathos, and the main narrative line is enriched or disrupted, depending on the reader's tastes, by stories within stories within stories. Along with the familiar stylistic choices and narrative elements, Erdrich's thematic concerns, particularly in *Books and Islands,* reveal an ongoing commitment to addressing colonial issues even in her nonfiction. *The Blue Jay's Dance* is more inward-looking: the text explores the author's physical, emotional, and spiritual life during pregnancy and after childbirth. Erdrich draws a tight circumference around herself and her family, sparingly sharing specifics of her everyday life. While it would seem to be the more personal of her two nonfiction works, considering that it discusses parts of her life with her children and Michael Dorris, its subject matter ranging across motherhood, family, nature, comfort food, childhood, pregnancy, sex, love, and home, Erdrich offers meditations on these subjects in a series of sketches rather than sharing intimate details of the Erdrich-Dorris household.

The Blue Jay's Dance is Erdrich's memoir recounting the pregnancy and birth of a baby, who is an amalgam of the three daughters she had with Michael Dorris.[8] The relationship between mothers and their children is the focus of the book. Readers anticipating sensational details of the inner workings of Erdrich's marriage to Dorris will be disappointed. Instead the processes, both emotional and biological, of pregnancy and motherhood, along with discussions of family histories, traditions, and the natural environment, make up the primary content of the book, in a very meaningful and vulnerable way for a writer who often guards her private life carefully. Erdrich divides the book into four parts: winter, spring, summer, and fall. For the Ojibwe everything has its time and season, and the cyclic nature of conception, pregnancy, birth, life, and death echoes the natural passing of time. The organizing principle ends there, however, as each seasonal section is divided into vignettes titled, for example, "Wintergardens," "In praise of my husband's hair," "Woodchuck punctuality," and "The newborn's dance." Erdrich shares stories of her grandparents, her childhood, her children, and her experience of the natural world and even family recipes. In fact there are more than ten complete recipes, with ingredient lists and directions, sprinkled throughout the text. "Dorris's lemon meringue pie," which he perfected as the only male in his childhood home and in the home he shared with Erdrich, is one of her favorite comfort foods, "guaranteed to cool and soothe irascible women" (16). Of course Erdrich's humor is always a feature of her writing, and she shares recipes for an "all-licorice dinner menu" (125) and her paternal grandmother's "hypothetical pierogies" (201). These recipes represent Dorris's attempts to calm her and cheer her up through nostalgic foods, though he "attempted the impossible—to replicate a childhood taste" (202). Throughout the text she describes her appreciation of his efforts to make her pregnancies as comfortable as possible. The moments between Erdrich and Dorris paint a picture of an idyllic life and offer a glimpse into their busy household while allowing Erdrich the space to describe her best memories of her married life and leave an artifact of that time for her children.

Erdrich weaves throughout the text various parts of her cultural heritage, but a specific moment she describes in "Grandpa's Prayer" marks a monumental episode in Erdrich's life, one in which her maternal grandfather, Patrice Gourneau, was remembered and honored. Gourneau is dressed in casual working-class attire: "old baggy jeans, leather boots, a green Sears work shirt, and a white T-shirt underneath" (187). His clothing belies the prominence he reached as tribal chairman in the Turtle Mountain Band of Ojibwe and the political clout he wielded in Washington, D.C., fighting for Ojibwe rights. Erdrich is fully aware of these accomplishments, but the lasting impression he left for his granddaughter was that "there was no end to his kindness, no end to the things only he could know" (187). Erdrich watches as he walks to the woods to pray, "carrying a leather-covered bone in his hand, a prayer bone, the hollowed foreleg of a deer into which he'd poured seeds, earth, all that he felt necessary to life" (187). Erdrich admits that "I couldn't understand him because he was praying in fluid Ojibwe, a language that sounds like water hitting the bottom of a boat" (187). As it turns out, in this significant moment, her grandfather is praying for her success. Erdrich's inclusion of this moment is not only to assert the prescience of her grandfather or the power of Ojibwe spirituality but also to illustrate the importance of the Ojibwe language in her upbringing and its role in her cultural heritage. Since Gourneau's death Erdrich has become a student of Ojibwe, and one can only surmise that one motivation to learn the language is to honor her grandfather's memory.

Erdrich explains the significance of the title of *The Blue Jay's Dance* in a section with the same title near the end of the work. Her observation of a blue jay dancing outside her window offers to her a metaphor for motherhood. When confronted with a hawk, the blue jay performs a frantic dance to scare it away, a mindless, instinctual effort to save her nest that involves potentially sacrificing herself for her children. The jay, "ridiculous, continues to dance, hopping forward, hornpiping up and down with tiny leaps, all of its feathers on end to increase its size" (194). The hawk "puzzles at the absurd display before she raises her wings and lifts off" (195). The fierce love of the mother in the face of death moves Erdrich to think of the sacrifices her ancestors made to protect and preserve their offspring. That mother love, self-sacrificing and sometimes suicidal, represents one of the greatest natural bonds seen on earth. Erdrich feels communion with the little jay as she watches the scene unfold outside her window, and she contemplates her baby and their own connection. She notes her baby's eyes, which "register me as a blurred self-extension" (195). Survival and preservation is the goal of a mother, and Erdrich takes lessons in motherhood where she will, from nature and from those family members who came before her. The essential quality of nature and the seasons in the lives of humans reflects the lasting values passed down from her Ojibwe ancestors.

Similarly in *Books and Islands in Ojibwe Country,* Erdrich privileges her Ojibwe ancestry, though in this work the occasion is not pregnancy but a road trip with her youngest daughter. As part of National Geographic's Literary Travel series, Erdrich's travelogue is much more in line with a memoir such as *The Blue Jay's Dance* than a tourists' guidebook of the region. *Books and Islands* is a thoughtful meditation on leaving home, traveling to one's ancestral lands, and returning home again. Throughout the work Erdrich offers reflections from a road trip through former Ojibwe territories in the upper Great Lakes region of northern Minnesota to southern Canada and various islands in the Lake of the Woods territory near the Red Lake reservation in present-day Ontario. Moving between discussions of her accompanying toddler, Nenaa'ikiizhikok, and the toddler's father, Tobasonakwut, Erdrich discusses family relationships, the Ojibwe language, sacred and historical places and monuments, and Ojibwe culture. Occasionally Erdrich also reveals the grievances she harbors against the greater Euro-American society responsible for the loss of Ojibwe land and the suppression of Ojibwe culture. Unlike *The Blue Jay's Dance, Books and Islands* reflects the twenty-first-century concerns and frustrations of a colonized subject moving through lands that were once part of a boundless Ojibwe territory.

While sharing aspects of her personal life, Erdrich creates a meaningful hybrid of travel literature, educational text, and memoir. The places she travels are not simply sites on a map but sacred places for the Ojibwe. Replete with personal sketches of rock paintings she encounters and traditional Ojibwe stories she hears during the trip, Erdrich's book recalls the Birchbark House series and its many teaching moments in its use and discussion of the Ojibwe language and the sacred nature of storytelling. After all the two ideas—books and islands—are symbolic of the two most vital aspects of Ojibwe culture to Erdrich, the language and the land. In her discussion of the various origins of the word *Ojibwe,* for instance, Erdrich explains that her favorite meaning of the word is from the verb *Ozhibii'ige,* which means "to write."[9] Not surprisingly she embraces this translation, and what a serendipitous meaning it is for a part-Ojibwe writer. Erdrich notes that "the Ojibwe people were great writers from way back and synthesized the oral and written tradition by keeping mnemonic scrolls of inscribed birchbark. The first paper, the first books" (11). Even the rock paintings found on various islands in the Lake of the Woods are a kind of writing—graphic representations of aspects of Ojibwe culture. "Lake of the Woods in Ontario and Minnesota has 14,000 islands. Some of them are painted islands, the rocks bearing signs ranging from a few hundred to more than a thousand years old" (3).The rock paintings serve as the mark of a people and a culture that has persisted through centuries, perhaps millennia, in the face of nature, war, colonization, and modern life. Erdrich views the ancient paintings as a testament to the survival of the Ojibwe.

Erdrich assumes a more political stance in *Books and Islands* than in *The Blue Jay's Dance.* An example is when she refers to Edward Curtis's and Ernest Oberholtzer's photographic documentation of Ojibwe life. Erdrich described the common misperception of Ojibwe attitudes toward being photographed: "Photographers did not take Ojibwe souls, it wasn't that easy. Soul theft required the systematic hard work of inventive humiliations and abuse by the government and by Catholic nuns and priests" (5). Erdrich is writing these words not in the voice of a fictional character but as herself. Her tone is at times overtly political when she views various Ojibwe artifacts and former territories. The island she makes her home base during her travels only has camp owners as its residents when by treaty rights the land should "still belong solely to the Ojibwe" (34). The mark of colonialism is also seen through Erdrich's eyes in the renaming of places. During her exploration of the territory, she visits a place the Ojibwe refer to as Spirit Bay, though on her map the Americans call it "Devil's Bay," which she finds "so tiresome and insulting" (5). The official record erases the Ojibwe spiritual denotation of the place in favor of a name that signifies an evil or non-Christian system of belief. Erdrich is confronted with a litany of insulting names for sacred Ojibwe places: "Squaw Rock. Devil's This and Devil's That. Indian or Tomahawk Anything" (5). She jokes that "some day, when there is nothing more important to do, the Anishinaabeg will demand that all the names be changed" (6). In a personal effort to preserve Ojibwe language and culture through naming, Erdrich chose a sacred Ojibwe name for her fourth daughter, eighteen-month-old Nenaa'ikiizhikok, who is traveling with her. The name comes from the spirit woman who "looks after the rains, the clouds, the storms, the waters in the sky" (12). The toddler, referred to as Kiizhikok, or "sky woman," through the rest of the text, shares the name with her paternal grandmother, the mother of Tobasonakwut, the child's father and Erdrich's partner at the time.

Tobasonakwut, a former Indian boarding school student, renowned healer, and political activist, embodies Ojibwe cultural history and spirit. Erdrich describes him as a "traditional healer, as well as a tribal politician, teacher, and negotiator . . . always being called on life or death missions. . . . He is a one-man spiritual ER" (23). The story of his childhood and his work as an Ojibwe elder statesman is the main vehicle by which Erdrich relates various aspects of traditional Ojibwe ways of being in the contemporary world. More pointedly Tobasonakwut symbolizes the survival of the Ojibwe through centuries of colonization and assimilation. The various assimilation practices of Western society had the ironic and unintended effect of instilling a profound desire in many Ojibwe to preserve their culture rather than adopting Western culture. Tobasonakwut is a case in point. He works tirelessly to provide his Ojibwe community with opportunities to practice traditional ceremonies and customs because of his Western education—the identity-stripping boarding school education he received as part of systematic assimilation practices. Sharing traditional stories with Erdrich, including that of his own history with the area, Tobasonakwut is characterized as a teacher for her more than a lover. The stories he shares range from before settlement of the area to after colonization, when clans of Ojibwe were removed to the reservations. In Ojibwe culture stories are used to teach practical lessons and to document history, and Tobasonakwut employs stories to the same end:

> Tobasonakwut grew up on a spit of land called Niiyaawaangashing, in a time before the Ojibwe or Anishinaabeg were removed from their homes in the islands. He is fortunate to know something of the time when his community was intact, when the bays were dotted with cabins and camps, when his extended family lived more or less by the spiritual seasons of the *Midewiwin,* the Grand Medicine teachings, and those ceremonial teachings form the moral and social center of the community. The teachings made sense of the beauties and hardships of Ojibwe existence. He was also unfortunate, for the world was devastated in just a few years. After his people had stabilized their lives and partly recovered from the wave of nineteenth-century invasions and diseases, the Canadian governments invented devastating aboriginal policies. It is his burden to have seen what survived of the Ojibwe world around him nearly demolished by death, removal, forced relocation, the poison of alcohol, and to have experienced an education that amounted to kidnapping and a brutal attempt at brainwashing. (33–34)

Tobasonakwut was not only an intimate friend of Erdrich's but also a source of tribal history and wisdom—a tribal elder for her to gain insights about her Ojibwe heritage. The gift of his stories, of firsthand accounts of preremoval, prereservation Ojibwe life on the islands, certainly was priceless for her creative work and her own ever-growing sense of Ojibwe identity and history. It is no surprise when, in an overtly political act of culture preservation, Erdrich reveals one way in which she exposes her daughter to the rich Ojibwe heritage of Tobasonakwut and remembers his identity-crippling boarding school education: "And then I pack a bag containing all of my baby's books, many of which I've laboriously blotted with Wite-Out, removing the English, and replaced with Ojibwe words written in Magic Markers" (10). Of course Erdrich is punning on *white* and the magic of Ojibwe, of the power of writing, and of taking back or decolonizing the education of her youngest.

Another recurring theme in Erdrich's writing is conservation. From her conversations with Tobasonakwut, she learns about the interrelatedness and integral connection of his people and her ancestors to their natural environment: "His people were the lake, and the lake was them. At one time, everyone who lived near the lake was essentially made of the lake. As the people lived off fish, animals, the lake's water and water plants for medicine, they were literally cell by cell composed of the lake and the lakes' islands. Tobasonakwut's father once said to him, *The creator is the lake and we are the waves on the lake*" (34). Though most inhabitants of any given place vaguely understand the connection between the land and the people, Tobasonakwut's innate belief in his clan's profound internalization of the landscape on a molecular level reveals the depth to which the Ojibwe were tied to the land. Erdrich notices this connection in Kiizh when some ancient magnetism draws the surrounding wildlife to the toddler during their trip: "The animals come close as if they want to get a good look at this child whose ancestors watched their ancestors, whose grandmother ate their grandmothers, whose father was stolen from among them by priests" (58). Erdrich is not only traveling the land of her ancestors but that of her children, particularly this daughter, whose time with her father is documented and memorialized for posterity.

Throughout the book Erdrich describes various stops on the road trip and, as the title suggests, a number of books she has encountered and holds dear. Her favorites range from Angela Carter's *Saints and Sinners* to her trusty *A Concise Dictionary of Minnesota Ojibwe* by John D. Nichols and Earl Nyholm to W. G. Sebald's *Austerlitz* to Henry James's *The Aspern Papers,* but one book stands out: *The Falcon, a Narrative of the Captivity and Adventures of John Tanner during Thirty Years Residence among the Indians in the Interior of North America.* During Erdrich's childhood, while spending time at her maternal grandparents' house in the summer, Tanner's narrative captured her imagination. The copy of *The Falcon* was read so often in the Erdrich household that it was falling apart at the seams. Erdrich recalls, "My sisters and I read this book in its old Ross and Haines edition until the spine gave, the pages tumbled out and were held together with a rubberband" (43). The section on Tanner is brief but of great significance in Erdrich's early reading life and her writing. Tanner himself did not have any Ojibwe ancestry; he was of Euro-American stock from Kentucky but was caught as a child by the Shawnee, "brought north, sold, adopted," and raised by an Ojibwe woman and her clan (43). As an adult, traveling in the same places Tanner describes in his narrative, Erdrich realizes that "it doesn't take much imagination to see myself in Tanner's world" (43). Her identification with Tanner, particularly as a mixed-blood Ojibwe, reveals her own desire to be part of a way of life that no longer exists. While Tanner expressed a desire to live among the Indians and circumstances brought him to that world, for Erdrich the old ways of the Ojibwe, their original way of life, exists only on reservations and in books.

Tanner's words have had an effect on Erdrich as a writer even into her adulthood. In her introduction to the Penguin Classics edition of *The Falcon,* she writes that "his life was a paradigmatic quest to belong, a restless search for peace and place" (xv). The restlessness in Erdrich's characters may be traced back to Tanner's own narrative. Peter J. Beidler argues that Tanner's influence on Erdrich's writing is clearly seen in novels such as *Tracks* and *The Birchbark*

House. He posits a central argument for Erdrich's use of Tanner in her own works: "One of the curious problems facing contemporary Native American fiction writers is how they learn about their people's history, and one of the curious solutions to this problem is that these writers turn to non-Indian authors to fill gaps in their knowledge about the history and traditions of early Indian peoples. It is ironic that the colonialist attitudes that ultimately led to the near obliteration of early Native ways of life and living oral traditions provide later Indians with written sources of information to which they would otherwise have no access."[10] While he makes salient points that many Native American writers had no other recourse than to look to non-Native writers for detailed information about daily life and that Tanner certainly influenced Erdrich, Beidler's argument discounts the oral tradition that Erdrich extols in her work. Stories and storytelling are prominently featured in her writing—not written stories but the Ojibwe's oral tradition. Erdrich surely heard stories through the years during time spent with various tribal elders in her childhood, including her grandfather Patrice Gourneau and her extended Ojibwe family, and as an adult, as illustrated in her recounting of Tobasonakwut's stories.

Books and Islands is not only historical or political. There are moments of great vulnerability in which Erdrich reveals intimate details of her life, including some of her most private insecurities. In moments of self-analysis, contemplating her late motherhood and Tobasonakwut's advanced age (approaching sixty), Erdrich reveals that "I'm too old to be a new mother, of course, and so's her dad. Our baby was born a great-aunt. But we won't get into that" (13). But she does get into it, merely by drawing attention to the logistics of the situation. Erdrich and her partner are in midlife with a toddler, and while the passing comment may seem insignificant, it expresses in a few words the very real concerns of a middle-aged mother regarding preparedness, mortality, and public perception. Erdrich is addressing a perceived public criticism or attitude. Even her mixed-blood heritage and position between the Ojibwe and non-Ojibwe worlds takes up her thoughts: "There was a time when I wondered—do I really believe all of this? I'm half German. Rational! Does this make any sense? After a while such questions stopped mattering" (16). Again it seems as if Erdrich is addressing a perceived public scrutiny about authenticity. She does not accept the position of "voice of the Ojibwe people," but through her considerable body of work, she gives readers one perspective of Ojibwe life, even though in some overly critical corners, her Ojibwe voice may be subject to unwarranted inspection.

Most affectingly, however, Erdrich describes how two of her brothers, Louis and Ralph, who both work in Ojibwe country, helped her through the aftermath of Michael Dorris's death in 1997. They "took off work to come and stay with me, to answer the telephone, and guard my children. They also made sure I didn't stay in bed all day, chew the woodwork, or just sit in the corner and drool" (22). Erdrich's debilitating pain over Dorris's suicide, however briefly touched upon, is clearly illustrated in these few lines. For someone so private, the laying bare of this grief speaks volumes about her relationship with Dorris, whatever controversy may have surrounded their marriage and his relationship with his children, both adopted and biological. Dorris was the father of Erdrich's three older daughters and her constant companion during her rise to literary fame, and her suffering over his untimely demise is poignant. These lines represent an intimate and authentic expression of Erdrich's mourning of him.

By the end of *Books and Islands*, Erdrich has returned to Minneapolis to her bookstore, Birchbark Books, an independent bookstore specializing in Ojibwe publications, to resume her everyday life. She also hints at the difficulty of maintaining a romantic relationship with Tobasonakwut: "He has a complicated life up north and I have a complicated life down in Minneapolis, so there is a lot of gigaa-waabamin" (89). Erdrich explains the Ojibwe tradition of not saying goodbye but rather *gigaa-waabamin*, "I'll see you again." Both Erdrich and Tobasonakwut had personal and professional obligations in their separate lives, and yet the relationship clearly remained one of deep and lasting friendship and respect, though it did not end in marriage. Tobasonakwut was an appropriate companion for Erdrich at this time in her life, when she was continuing to improve her comprehension of the Ojibwe language and had established herself as a steward of Ojibwe history and culture through her creative accomplishments. Ultimately *Books and Islands in Ojibwe Country* describes a meaningful road trip, a lifelong love affair with books, an intimate relationship with a beloved companion, and the ways in which these things reinforce Erdrich's commitment to preserving Ojibwe culture and language for future generations, including her own children.

NOTES

Chapter 1—Understanding Louise Erdrich

1. Established in the early nineteenth century, the BIA is the federal government's oversight agency for indigenous tribes. The BIA is charged with the administration of certain health, education, land management, and general welfare services.

2. Halliday, "Louise Erdrich."

3. Ibid.

4. George, "Interview with Louise Erdrich."

5. Williams, "Three Graces."

6. Bruchac, "Whatever Is Really Yours."

7. Gates, *Faces of America,* 81.

8. Ibid., 82.

9. Erdrich, foreword to *First Person, First People,* xiii.

10. Ibid., xii.

11. Ibid., x.

12. Ibid.

13. Halliday, "Louise Erdrich."

14. Berkley, "PW Interviews."

15. Halliday, "Louise Erdrich."

16. Tazioli, "Louise Erdrich."

17. Louise Erdrich, "Louise Erdrich ND 2013 Rough Riders Award Ceremony," Prairie Public, April 19, 2013, http://www.prairiepublic.org/television/prairie-public-on-demand/read-north-dakota-presents/louise-erdrich-nd-2013-rough-rider-award-ceremony.

18. The Ojibwe word *chimookoman,* a metonymic word referencing the long swords carried by the Europeans, translates literally as "big knife."

19. For examples in Western literature, see René de Chateaubriand's *Atala* (1801) and *René* (1802), James Fenimore Cooper's *Last of the Mohicans* (1826), Mary Rowlandson's captivity narrative, and much of American frontier literature. Television has its famous stock Native American characters, for example, Tonto from *The Lone Ranger,* as well.

20. Silko, "Here's an Odd Artifact," 179.

21. Ibid.

22. Chavkin and Chavkin, *Conversations,* 237.

23. Pérez Castillo, "Postmodernism," 288.

24. Petersen, "History, Postmodernism," 983.

25. Gerald Vizenor, "American Indian Art and Literature Today: Survivance and Tragic Wisdom," *Museum International* 62, no. 3 (2010): 43–46.

26. Pérez Castillo, "Postmodernism," 294.

27. Louise Erdrich, e-mail to the author, March 6, 2014.

28. Ibid.

29. Ibid.

30. Ibid.

31. Ibid.

32. Moyers, "Louise Erdrich," 23.

Chapter 2—*Love Medicine, The Bingo Palace,* and *The Painted Drum*

1. Lincoln, introduction, xi.

2. Ibid., xv–xvi.

3. Erdrich, "Author's Note," in *Love Medicine,* 6. All subsequent page references will be given parenthetically in the text and refer to the New York: Harper Perennial, 2009, edition.

4. Erdrich, e-mail to author, March 6, 2014.

5. Erdrich, *Bingo Palace,* 5. All subsequent page references will be given parenthetically in the text and refer to the New York: Harper Perennial, 2006, edition.

6. Erdrich, *Painted Drum,* 59. All subsequent page references will be given parenthetically in the text and refer to the New York: Harper Perennial, 2006, edition.

7. See Andrea Smith, "Boarding School Abuses, Human Rights, and Reparations," *Social Justice* 31, no. 4 (1998): 90. Smith states that "the rationale for choosing cultural rather than physical genocide was often economic": the cost to pursue military campaigns against the Indians over a ten-year period was $22 million, while the cost of educating thirty thousand children over ten years was a quarter of that amount.

8. Anton Treuer, *Ojibwe in Minnesota* (Saint Paul: Minnesota Historical Society Press, 2009), 31–33.

9. The chapter first appeared as a short story in the *New Yorker*, which is a common practice for Erdrich. She often develops the seeds of a novel in a short story and then expands the story into a novel.

Chapter 3—*Tracks, Four Souls,* and *The Last Report on the Miracles at Little No Horse*

1. Stead, "Unlocking the Tale," 41.

2. Williams, "Facing the World," proclaimed that "*Tracks* may be the story of our time" (2). Kakutani, "Books of the Times," extolled Erdrich's "gift for locating the intersection between public and private grief" and noted that what in another author's hand might seem "melodramatic" or "mundane" is propelled "into the magical and eternal world of fable."

3. Cryer, "Broken Spirits."

4. Louise Erdrich, *Tracks,* 31. All subsequent page references will be given parenthetically in the text and refer to the New York: HarperCollins, 1989, edition.

5. Scott, *Gamefulness of American Postmodernism,* 120.

6. See Gerald Vizenor's *Narrative Chance: Postmodern Discourse on Native American Literature* (1989) and *The People Named Ojibwe: Narrative Histories* (1984) for discussions of the postmodern implications of Native American storytelling and the notion of "survivance." Also informative is Sister Bernard, Ellen Frogner, and Estelle Eich's *Ojibwa Myths and Legends* (1962) for a discussion of the sacred role of storytelling in Ojibwe culture.

7. Erdrich, *Four Souls,* 4. All subsequent page references will be given parenthetically in the text and refer to the New York: Harper Perennial, 2005, edition.

8. "Gakaabikaang," in *The Ojibwe People's Dictionary,* In *The Ojibwe People's Dictionary,* http://ojibwe.lib.umn.edu/main-entry/gakaabikaang-name-place (accessed February 14, 2015).

9. Father Jude is the estranged youngest brother of Mary and Karl Adare and the uncle of Dot Adare. The Adares are central characters in *The Beet Queen.*

10. Many of Erdrich's previous characters contribute to the narrative; Lulu Nanapush, Marie Lazarre, and Margaret Kashpaw all figure in Father Damien's reports.

11. Erdrich, *Last Report on the Miracles,* 74. All subsequent page references will be listed parenthetically in the text and refer to the New York: Harper Perennial, 2009, edition.

Chapter 4—*The Plague of Doves* and *The Round House*

1. The short stories are not discussed apart from the novels, as Erdrich incorporates the majority of them into her longer works of fiction.

2. Moyers, "Louise Erdrich," 22.

3. Nance, "Never the Same River Twice," 50.

4. Erdrich, *Shadow Tag,* 7. All subsequent page references will be listed parenthetically in the text and refer to the New York: HarperCollins, 2010, edition.

5. See Beidler, *Murdering Indians.* The historical event is fully investigated in Beidler's study.

6. Erdrich, *Plague of Doves,* 297. All subsequent page references will be given parenthetically in the text and refer to the New York: Harper Perennial, 2009, edition.

7. Erdrich, "About the Book: From Mustache Maude to 9/11, the Story behind the Book," in *Plague of Doves,* 6–7. In this short piece, part of the supplemental material included in the "P.S." sections of the Harper Perennial paperback editions of her novels, Erdrich writes about certain themes and contexts of the novel.

8. Duthu, "Louise Erdrich."

9. Ibid.

10. Erdrich, "Rape on the Reservation."

11. Ibid.

12. Erdrich, *Round House,* 161. All subsequent page references will be given parenthetically in the text and refer to the New York: HarperCollins, 2012, edition.

13. Hansen, "In 'House.'"

14. Nance, "Never the Same River Twice," 51.

15. Hansen, "In 'House.'"

Chapter 5—The Birchbark House Series

1. See Papazian, "Razing Little Houses," for a comparison of Wilder's Little House series and Erdrich's children's books.

2. Rochman, "Little House on the Lake."

3. Erdrich has planned seven to ten volumes for the series.

4. Erdrich, "Thanks and Acknowledgements," in *Birchbark House.* All subsequent page references will be given parenthetically in the text and refer to the New York: Hyperion Books for Children, 1999, edition.

5. Linda Hutcheon, e-mail message to author, September 7, 2013. Referring to Erdrich's adult fiction, Hutcheon believes much of her work could be characterized as "historiographic fiction."

6. Rochman, "Little House on the Lake," 1427.

7. The term *removal* refers to the Indian Removal Act of 1830, enacted by the federal government to displace Native American tribes from the east to west of the Mississippi. The Ojibwes avoided this forced relocation until 1850, when President Zachary Taylor, bowing to pressure from Euro-American settlers in the upper Midwest, ordered their removal.

8. Erdrich, *Game of Silence,* xii. All subsequent page references will be given parenthetically in the text and refer to the New York: Harper Trophy, 2006, edition.

9. Wisconsin Historical Society, "Sandy Lake Tragedy," August 13, 2013, http://www.wisconsinhistory.org/dictionary/index.asp?action=view&term_id=500&term_type_id=3&term_type_text=things.

10. Chrysostom Verwyst, "Frederic Baraga," in *The Catholic Encyclopedia,* vol. 2 (New York: Appleton, 1907), http://www.newadvent.org/cathen/02282b.htm (accessed October 2, 2013).

11. Erdrich, *Porcupine Year,* xi. All subsequent page references will be given parenthetically in the text and refer to the New York: HarperCollins, 2010, edition.

12. During this time both the Sand Creek massacre in 1864 and the Sioux uprising occurred, which resulted in the largest mass execution in U.S. history, ordered by President Lincoln.

13. Erdrich, *Chickadee,* 87. All subsequent page references will be given parenthetically in the text.

Chapter 6—Poetry and Nonfiction

1. Halliday, "Louise Erdrich."

2. Bruchac, "Whatever Is Really Yours."

3. Alison Lurie, ed., *The Oxford Book of Modern Fairy Tales* (Oxford: Oxford University Press, 1993), xvii.

4. Erdrich, *Baptism of Desire,* 48. All subsequent page references will be given parenthetically in the text and refer to the New York: Harper Perennial, 2001, edition.

5. Jaskoski, review of *Baptism of Desire,* 55.

6. Erdrich, *Original Fire,* 51. All subsequent page references will be given parenthetically in the text and refer to the New York: Harper Perennial, 2004, edition.

7. Erdrich, introduction to *The Falcon,* xii.

8. Erdrich, *Blue Jay's Dance,* ix. This page reference refers to the New York: Harper Perennial, 2010, edition.

9. Erdrich, *Books and Islands,* 11. All subsequent page references will be given parenthetically in the text.

10. Beidler, "Facts of Fictional Magic," 37.

SELECTED BIBLIOGRAPHY

Works by Louise Erdrich

FICTION

Love Medicine. New York: Holt, 1984. Expanded ed., New York: HarperCollins, 1993; revised, 2009.
The Beet Queen. New York: Holt, 1986.
Tracks. New York: HarperCollins, 1988.
The Crown of Columbus. With Michael Dorris. New York: HarperCollins, 1991.
The Bingo Palace. New York: HarperCollins, 1994.
Tales of Burning Love. New York: HarperCollins, 1996.
The Antelope Wife. New York: HarperCollins, 1998; revised, 2012.
The Last Report on the Miracles at Little No Horse. New York: HarperCollins, 2001.
The Master Butchers Singing Club. New York: HarperCollins, 2003.
Four Souls. New York: HarperCollins, 2004.
The Painted Drum. New York: HarperCollins, 2005.
The Red Convertible: Selected and New Stories, 1978–2008. New York: HarperCollins, 2009.
The Plague of Doves. New York: HarperCollins, 2009.
Shadow Tag. New York: HarperCollins, 2010.
The Round House. New York: HarperCollins, 2012.

POETRY

Jacklight. New York: Holt, 1984.
Baptism of Desire. New York: HarperCollins, 1989.
Original Fire: New and Selected Poems. New York: HarperCollins, 2003.

CHILDREN'S FICTION

Grandmother's Pigeon. Illustrated by Jim LaMarche, New York: Hyperion Books for Children, 1996.
The Birchbark House. New York: Hyperion Books for Children, 1999.
The Range Eternal. Illustrated by Steve Johnson and Lou Fancher. New York: Hyperion Book for Children, 2002.
The Game of Silence. New York: HarperCollins, 2004.
The Porcupine Year. New York: HarperCollins, 2008.
Chickadee. New York: HarperCollins, 2012.

NONFICTION

Imagination. New York: Merrill, 1980. A textbook for children.

Route 2. With Michael Dorris. Northridge, Cal.: Lord John, 1981. Travel literature.

The Blue Jay's Dance: A Birth Year. New York: HarperCollins, 1995.

Books and Islands in Ojibwe Country: Traveling in the Land of My Ancestors. Washington, D.C.: National Geographic, 2003.

OTHER WORKS

Foreword to *The Broken Cord: A Family's Ongoing Struggle with Fetal Alcohol Syndrome*, by Michael Dorris. New York: Harper, 1989, xi–xix.

Editor, *The Best American Short Stories of 1993*. New York: Houghton Mifflin, 1993.

Foreword to *First Person, First Peoples: Native American College Graduates Tell Their Life Stories*, edited by Andrew Garrod and Colleen Larimore, ix–xiii. Ithaca, N.Y.: Cornell University Press, 1997.

Introduction to *The Falcon: A Narrative of the Captivity and Adventures of John Tanner*, by John Tanner, xi–xv. New York: Penguin, 1994.

Winter Reader 2003–2004. Minneapolis: Center for Book Arts, 2003. Limited edition chapbook.

Introduction to *Winter in the Blood*, by James Welch. New York: Penguin Classics, 2008.

Foreword to *Lines from a Mined Mind: The Words of John Trudell*, by John Trudell, vii. Golden, Colo.: Fulcrum, 2008.

"The Years of My Birth." *New Yorker*, January 10, 2011, 65. Short fiction.

Foreword to *Every Day Is a Good Day: Reflections by Contemporary Indigenous Women, Memorial Edition*, by Wilma Mankiller, ix-x. Golden, Colo.: Fulcrum, 2011.

"Ringo's Gold." *New Yorker*, November 21, 2011, 104. Nonfiction piece.

"Nero." *New Yorker*, May 7, 2012, 60. Short fiction.

"Voting in Little Earth." *New Yorker Online*, November 8, 2012. http://www.newyorker.com/online/blogs/newsdesk/2012/11/voting-in-little-earth.html. Opinion piece.

"Rape on the Reservation." *New York Times*, Opinion Pages, February 26, 2013. http://www.nytimes.com/2013/02/27/opinion/native-americans-and-the-violence-against-women-act.html?r=1&. Opinion piece.

"The Big Cat." *New Yorker*, March 31, 2014. http://www.newyorker.com/fiction/features/2014/03/31/140331fi_fiction_erdrich.

SELECTED INTERVIEWS

Berkley, Miriam. "PW Interviews: Louise Erdrich." *Publishers Weekly*, August 15, 1986, 58–59. An early review discussing Erdrich's background and her collaboration with Michael Dorris, particularly interesting as Dorris was present for the interview and interjects occasionally.

Bruchac, Joseph. "Whatever Is Really Yours." In *Survival This Way: Interviews with American Indian Poets*. Tucson: Sun Tracks/University of Arizona Press, 1987. 73–86. Bruchac, a Native American writer himself, interviews Erdrich about her Ojibwe cultural identity and several poems in *Jacklight*.

Chavkin, Allan, and Nancy Feyl Chavkin, eds. *Conversations with Louise Erdrich and Michael Dorris*. Jackson: University Press of Mississippi, 1994. The text collects more than twenty Erdrich and Dorris interviews, given both as a couple and singly.

Duthu, N. Bruce. "Louise Erdrich: A Reading and a Conversation." Montgomery Fellow Lecture. Moderated by N. Bruce Duthu. Dartmouth College, May 22, 2012 (online video, http://www.dartmouth.edu/~nas/events/). Erdrich returned to her alma mater, Dartmouth College, as Montgomery Fellow for the 2011–12 academic year. During her residence she gave a reading from *The Round House* and was interviewed by law professor N. Bruce Duthu about various aspects of the novel and Native American law.

George, Jan. "An Interview with Louise Erdrich." *North Dakota Quarterly* 53, no. 2 (1985): 240–47. An early review focused on Erdrich's background and the poems in *Jacklight*.

Halliday, Lisa. "Louise Erdrich, The Art of Fiction No. 208." *Paris Review* 195 (2010), http://www.theparisreview.org/interviews/6055/the-art-of-fiction-no-208-louise-erdrich. The most open and revealing interview Erdrich has granted to date. No subject is off-limits, including her marriage to and collaboration with Michael Dorris.

Hansen, Lianne. "In 'House,' Erdrich Sets Revenge on a Reservation." *All Things Considered*, October 2, 2012, http://www.npr.org/2012/10/02/162086064/in-house-erdrich-sets-revenge-on-a-reservation. The interview probes questions of law, justice, and sovereignty in *The Round House*.

Nance, Kevin. "Never the Same River Twice." *Poets and Writers Magazine*, November–December 2012, 49–55. Nance's comprehensive interview includes discussions of Erdrich's novels to date, her goals as a writer, and certain aspects of her personal life.

Rochman, Hazel. "Little House on the Lake." *Booklist*, April 1, 1999, 1427. Erdrich speaks about the relationship between her family history and *The Birchbark House* and addresses Laura Ingalls Wilder's *Little House on the Prairie* series.

Tazioli, Terry. "Louise Erdrich: *The Round House*." *Well Read TV*, Washington Public Affairs Network and KBTC, http://www.wellreadtv.com/louise-erdrich-the-round-house, accessed January 20, 2014. Erdrich discusses various themes and characters from *The Round House* as well as biographical information.

SELECTED CRITICISM AND REVIEWS

Beidler, Peter. "The Facts of Fictional Magic: John Tanner as a Source for Louise Erdrich's *Tracks* and *The Birchbark House*." *American Indian Culture and Research Journal* 24, no. 4 (2000): 37–54. Beidler analyzes the influence of John Tanner's *The Falcon* on some of Erdrich's historical fiction.

———. *Murdering Indians: A Documentary History of the 1897 Killings That Inspired Louise Erdrich's "The Plague of Doves."* Jefferson, N.C.: McFarland, 2013.

Cryer, Dan. "Broken Spirits on the Dakota Plains." Review of *Tracks* by Louise Erdrich. *Newsday*, September 4, 1988, 19. Cryer's lukewarm review of *Tracks* critiques Erdrich's narrative style.

Gates, Henry Louis, Jr. "Louis Erdrich." *Faces of America*. New York: New York University Press, 2010: 72–90. Gates conducts genealogical research on Erdrich's family and uncovers interesting parts of her Ojibwe, German, and French ancestry.

Jaskoski, Helen. Review of *Baptism of Desire: Poems*, by Louise Erdrich. *SAIL: Studies in American Indian Literatures*, 2d ser., 3, no. 4 (1991): 55–57. Jaskoski's favorable review of Erdrich's second poetry collection provides a helpful overview of the poems and highlights the religious aspects of the volume.

Kakutani, Michiko. "Books of the Times: Indians Displaced by Time and Loss." Review of *Tracks* by Louise Erdrich. *New York Times*, August 24, 1988, http://www.nytimes.com/1988/08/24/books/books-of-the-times-indians-displaced-by-time-and-loss.html.

Kakutani's early review exemplifies the positive reception Erdrich has enjoyed from established literary critics.

Lincoln, Kenneth. Preface to *Native American Renaissance*. Berkeley: University of California Press, 1985: xi–xvi. Though Lincoln's early study focuses more closely on other Native American authors, his prescient introduction presents Erdrich as an up-and-coming force in Native American letters.

Moyers, Bill. "Louise Erdrich." In *Bill Moyers Journal: The Conversation Continues,* 21–31. New York: New Press, 2011. Moyers has interviewed Erdrich numerous times over the course of her career, while she was with Michael Dorris and since. In this interview Erdrich shares her ideas on family, motherhood, Ojibwe spirituality, and language.

Papazian, Gretchen. "Razing Little Houses or Re-envisionary History: Louise Erdrich's Story of the American Frontier in *The Birchbark House* and *The Game of Silence*." In *Studies in the Literary Achievement of Louise Erdrich, Native American Writer*, edited by Brajesh Sawhney, 187–211. London: Mellen, 2008. Papazian offers a comparative analysis of Erdrich's Birchbark House series as a counternarrative to Laura Ingalls Wilder's Little House on the Prairie series.

Pérez Castillo, Susan. "Postmodernism, Native American Literature, and the Real: The Silko-Erdrich Controversy." *Massachusetts Review* 32, no. 2 (1991): 285–94. Pérez Castillo provides a rebuttal to Leslie Marmon Silko's unfavorable review of Erdrich's *The Beet Queen*.

Petersen, Nancy J. "History, Postmodernism, and Louise Erdrich's *Tracks*." *PMLA* 109 (1994): 982–94. Petersen's groundbreaking essay reveals the quandary for ethnic writers, particularly in a postmodern era, to provide authentic representation for underrepresented communities.

Scott, Steven D. *The Gamefulness of American Postmodernism: John Barth and Louise Erdrich*. New York: Lang, 2000. Scott presents Erdrich's narrative style and content in terms of game playing, in the same vein as John Barth's postmodern creative fiction.

Silko, Leslie Marmon. "Here's an Odd Artifact for the Fairy Tale Shelf." Review of *The Beet Queen* by Louise Erdrich. *SAIL: Studies in American Indian Literatures* 10 (Fall 1986): 178–184. Silko's oft-quoted review disparages what she perceives of postmodern narrative strategies at the cost of authentic political engagement.

Stead, Deborah. "Unlocking the Tale." Review of *Tracks* by Louise Erdrich. *New York Times Book Review* (Oct 02, 1988): 41. Stead offers an insightful review of the style and thematic concerns of Erdrich's *Tracks*.

Washburn, Frances. *Tracks on a Page: Louise Erdrich, Her Life and Works*. Santa Barbara, Calif.: Praeger, 2013. Washburn's study is a literary biography, tracing events of Erdrich's life and connecting them with her publications.

Williams, Sarah T. "The Three Graces." *Minneapolis Star Tribune,* February 4, 2008, http://www.startribune.com/entertainment/books/15083971.html. Williams's profile of Erdrich and two of her sisters includes insights from their parents, Ralph and Rita Erdrich, and examples of correspondence between Erdrich and her father.

Williams, Terry Tempest. "Facing the World without Land to Call Home." Review of *Tracks* by Louise Erdrich. *Los Angeles Times,* September 11, 1988, 2. Tempest offers a glowing review of *Tracks* in this early review.

INDEX

All unattributed titles are by Erdrich.

ABOUT THE AUTHOR

SEEMA KURUP is a professor of English at William Rainey Harper College. She received her Ph.D. in English from Kent State University, where her research interests focused on postmodern American literature and theory and multicultural women's literature. Her prior publications include book chapters on postmodern American literature and composition, as well as reference essays on various figures in twentieth century American literature.